# DIAMONDS IN OUR DAYS

## DISCOVERING GOD'S HEALING HOPE AND BEAUTY

## LISA WILT

**Diamonds In Our Days: Discovering Healing Hope and Beauty**

**Cover photo by Anderson Photography**

# DEDICATION

God never said a diamond was precious
or worthy of His love.
But **YOU** are.

**Isaiah 43:4 "You are precious to me.
You are honored, and I love you."**

This book is dedicated to our God who sees
beyond our lumps of coal to show us
**Diamonds In Our Days,**
a sample of what is to come in heaven.

# ACKNOWLEDGEMENTS

*S*ome mornings are difficult but this morning everything was brighter when I woke up, quite literally. The intensity of light drew me to my bedroom window and what I saw took my breath away.

God had unexpectedly decorated my world outside with shimmering snow. And if that weren't enough, He draped the trees with icicles that glistened like diamonds. I opened the door and inhaled the beauty.

Life stood still in that pure moment.

It's as if God was excited to show me that with Him an imperfect world filled with heartbreak and health crisis can have stunningly beautiful moments.

The cover of this book is my little piece of the world covered in sparkling beauty. The air is crystal clear. As far as my eyes can see, there is splendor. But before I head outside to make snow angels, I have a few people who have been angels to me and need to be thanked:

**\*Reverend Mike Costanzo** - You took a manuscript that was a diamond in the rough and helped polish it so it shines with Biblical clarity.

**\*Sue Steen and Jonna Beenken**–Like Carat, Color, Clarity and Cut make a diamond brilliant, you make this book glisten.

**\*My Heavenly Father**–Bigger than the Hope Diamond is my love for you. I am grateful for an eternity to show my gratitude.

**\*My Diamond Besties**–I've heard it said: "Diamonds are a girl's best friend." Not so for me. You all are. Thank you for sharing your sparkles and your lives: Dawn Anderson, Lynn Arnold, Sharon Baker, Kristen Bomgardner, Rosie Borre, Judy Chandler, Gloria Costanzo, Bee Culver, Lesli Cutshall, Barb DeBusk, Traci Dryer, Chris Durst, Phyllis Elliott, Bill Ellwood, Amanda Enloe, Cheryl Eustis, Alyssa Falck, Debby Falck, Kelly Grissom, Angie Hamilton, Amanda Hanna, Elaine Hanshaw, Rachel Jensen, Georgia Johnson, Sue Jones, Carla Kincaid, Christa Lane, Roxanne Lilly, Ceil Lynch, Lisa Mansfield, Natalie Michaels, Kathy Nale, Therese Nichols, Chris Nees, Kelly Ogle, Janice Reyburn, Mary Rosenquist, Cyndi Scarlett, Kim Shelton, Roxanne Smith, Sue Steen, Shelly Trear, Lisa Trueblood, Anne Wagner, Angie Williams and Diana Wuller.

# INTRODUCTION

*A* diamond is brilliant and beautiful...but it certainly doesn't start that way. Like an ugly lump of coal, a diamond is made of carbon. Yet after thousands of years with millions of pounds of pressure at insanely intense temperatures, carbon emerges beautifully transformed into a diamond.

But it is a "diamond in the rough." Only the diamond cutter clearly sees what the gem can become. He studies the precious stone and takes every detail into account before beginning his delicate work. Then painstakingly, facets are formed accenting the stone's natural beauty.

Flaws are minimized and the diamond's value skyrockets. The artisan understands that cutting, grinding and polishing leads to splendor. His work of art is exquisite and expensive, given to express enduring love.

Our Heavenly Father is our Master Artisan. He created you

and me and desires that every life experience gives us dimension. We are multi-faceted. You and I are beloved, brilliant and beautiful in God's eyes.

There are millions of diamonds but only one you. Though you may have wintery seasons when you feel more like a forgotten lump of coal, know that you are cherished and infinitely valuable.

It's no coincidence that diamonds are among the hardest substances on earth.[1] They are scratch resistant and nearly indestructible. Together with other carbon atoms, they have endured an epic journey through crushing conditions. Their atoms have bonded together becoming saturated and strong, forming a lattice work of carbon.

Together as women we have endured difficulties. While we each have experienced unique journeys, we too can bond together in faith. This provides us with renewed strength.

I know firsthand that some of life's hardest trials are health related. I've survived cancer scares and major surgeries. In all these hard things God assures us that He will bring good things (Romans 8:28). This is an eternal promise with everlasting implications.

On our faith expedition, we will discover how God transforms difficult things into gorgeous, glorious things so that you and I can emerge more resilient with spirits that radiate hope.

Working as a pharmacist, I see sickness daily. Honestly, it makes me question why God allows suffering. Are there deeper spiritual truths that can be mined from physical trials? What beauty can emerge from these life events?

How can we overcome pain, even when it's invisible to doctors who question our symptoms? How can we be more than conquerors when cancer threatens to knock us down and scare us silly?

What can gluten possibly teach us about grace? What can we learn about being joyful and content from restless legs syndrome? Might the plaque on our teeth encourage us to brush pride from our lives? What does Tylenol® have to teach us about living out truth? Might dyslexia help us to see sin and circumstances more clearly?

How could the common cold help us better understand Christ's uncommon gift of grace? Is it possible that our foot falling asleep could lead us to walk in faith living and giving more generously?

How do we make better food and life choices and what do a handful of potato chips have in common with a headful of recognition? And finally, what lessons on abiding might we learn from our belly buttons? (Yes, you read that right...our belly buttons.)

These are a few snapshots of the journey before us. It's going to be a fun adventure while we mine for rich spiritual truths. I love to laugh so hard I snort and our Great Physician prescribes it. He tells us that a merry heart is good for our soul (Proverbs 17:22). Science tells us that people who laugh more live longer.[2]

So here's to a life of healing hope and beauty. God, who has started a good work in us, promises to finish it (Philippians 1:6). So we, like the Hope Diamond, can be known for our opulent beauty.

Let's shine, transfusing others with hope. And for heaven's sake, let's be known for our love, helping others through hard times. Like diamonds, we can serve a higher purpose when we allow ourselves to be used by God.

Diamonds are not only stunning, they have purpose. Within the medical community, scientists are experimenting with the use of microscopic nanodiamonds within the human body. These diamonds are a hundred thousand times thinner than a strand of our hair. Diamonds are nontoxic, so they're safe to use internally.

They can safely coat our digestive tract. By applying a thin layer of sugar proteins, these tiny diamonds can pass through the walls of our intestine and attach themselves to specific types of cells. Oncologists can isolate cancer cells, white blood cells, or even damaged, precancerous tissue.

This diamond research will likely lead to their use in advanced medical imaging, but their potential is much more far-reaching. Once biologists work out a way to deliver these minuscule diamonds to specific areas of the body, they can be used for much more than just imaging.

Diamonds can deliver medicines to exact areas of the body, improving treatment options for everything from infections to cancer. They could also be used to track stem cells. With enough time and research, this may allow doctors to improve immune responses and regrow damaged nerves. While these advances may still be years away, they wouldn't be possible without the use of diamonds.[3]

Like nanodiamonds, we may feel small, but we can have a

huge impact on those around us. We too are called to deliver healing hope to others. We each long for meaning and purpose... and we want to know that our suffering counts for something and our lives matter to someone.

So in the end the hard things that God allows in our lives help us to more clearly understand the pain of those experiencing similar circumstances. Hard trials help provide clarity about what's most important in life. Clarity makes us and diamonds more gorgeous and infinitely more valuable.

So are you ready to turn the page and get started? Together let's ask God to bless this faith expedition as we seek to discover **Diamonds In Our Days!**

# A GOWN BUT NO GROOM

*H*e purposed! She accepted.

Time stood frozen in that perfect instant…a Fermata hold of sorts in a symphony of happily-ever-after.

Sophia was radiant with a flawless ivory complexion and a captivating smile. Her blonde tresses flowed effortlessly to her waist. Joyful engagement photos were taken. Save-the-date cards were sent. With her mom by her side, Sophia said YES to the dress!

The church was reserved and the reception deposit was made. Sophia selected rich hues of cranberries for her bridesmaids and booked a florist. Even the bubbles were bought for the reception departure.

Her fiancé was a man of faith. Sophia met Daniel her first week of college. He was her first serious boyfriend.

When he shared his testimony, she instantly began to fall in love. Daniel was a math major with a scruffy, full beard. He loved Sophia and the great outdoors.

She was so happy. It seemed a perfect match...like it was meant to be. Then the diagnosis was made. All her pain was finally given a name.

**L-u-p-u-s.** Five letters that injected four letters into Daniel's heart.

**F-e-a-r.** Four letters that led to a broken engagement. And then to five more letters that pierced deeper than any needle Sophia had ever known.

**A-l-o-n-e.** She felt alone.

Lupus gives a name to a difficult constellation of conditions; the immune system becomes a hyperactive villain, attacking perfectly healthy cells–the very cells it was designed to protect. The symptoms are widespread and can be stealth-like, attacking the heart, lungs, kidneys, skin and joints.

While the symptoms vary, almost every lupus patient has joint pain from inflammation. It affects more women than men and is most commonly diagnosed in early adulthood as it was with Sophia. 5,000,000 people worldwide (not counting those who love them) have known the fear that accompanies the diagnosis of Lupus.[1]

YOU MAY NOT HAVE LUPUS, BUT WHAT INJECTS FEAR INTO YOUR veins? Fear is a four-letter word that forges forward fast when we feel alone. I've heard it said that there are two ways to react to fear. **F.E.A.R.** is the acronym that spells out the options. We can

- Forget Everything And Run or
- Face Everything And Rise.[2]

So how do we, like sweet Sophia, rise above fear so we can keep breathing when life hurts? We begin by recognizing that fear is a feeling. It's a normal response when we face the unknown, especially when we face the unknown alone.

Feeling alone facing the unknown. Say that five times in the dark with a diagnosis for which there is no cure.

Sophia's fiancé fled from fear.

Now maybe you've never experienced a broken engagement, but have you ever experienced a broken heart? How about a

broken home…

broken dreams or…

broken health?

How do you spell fear? And when do you feel most alone?

Sometimes life is lonely and our heart aches. Jesus knew this. So before He left this Earth, He reminded us we will always have a Friend. This Companion will help us remember all we have been taught. In *John 14:26-27 he says:

> "I'm leaving you well and whole.
>
> That's my parting gift to you.
>
> **Peace.**

I don't leave you the way you're used to being left—
feeling abandoned, bereft.
**So don't be upset. Don't be distraught.**"

Have you ever *felt* abandoned and needed a friend? I have. Have you *felt* distraught? I was when I learned about Sophia, who has a gown but no groom.

Have you ever *felt* bereft, mourning every morning? I have been there more times than I want to remember. I have *felt* all these things and simultaneously had *faith* in the fact that I am NOT alone! I have a Friend–our Comforter.

Timothy was a similar age to Sophia's fiancé when Paul (his mentor in the faith) reminds him that "God has not given us a spirit of fear and timidity, but of power, love, and self-discipline (2 Timothy 1:7). "

With my Friend by my side, the darkness of fear must flee... like darkness when the light switch is flipped on. I remind myself of God's promise. He tells us if we look to Him and don't get worked up about what may or may not happen, He'll help us deal with the hurt, when and if it comes (Matthew 6:34).

If I am totally forthright, I'll tell you it's very easy for me to worry. Yet I do know that God is faithful and trustworthy. And He promises that He will help me with whatever hard things I may have to face...when the time comes.

It's a moment-by-moment, step-by-step challenge to walk in faith. Fear is a feeling...a natural feeling innate to our flesh. I choose to walk by faith, not by a feeling. By faith I will be a WARRIOR, not a WORRIER! Let's do this together!

THE JOURNEY FORWARD:

Fiancés may flee from fear but our Friend is always faithful. And there is hope. The first new drug in fifty years has just been approved for the treatment of Lupus.

For nearly 3,000 years we've had the treatment for fear. It can be found in *Isaiah 43:1-3: "Don't be afraid, I've redeemed you. I've called your name. You're mine. When you're in over your head, I'll be there with you. When you're in rough waters, you will not go down. When you're between a rock and a hard place, it won't be a dead end—because I am God, your personal God, The Holy One of Israel, your Savior. I paid a price for you."

And for those of us who like happy endings, I'm excited to share that Sophia graduated from college and landed a terrific job as a journalist and has a new love.

# RING AROUND MY FINGER

## THE DARK SMUDGE

On our faith expedition to mine **Diamonds In Our Days**, I've looked at the diamond in my wedding setting a bit more often. Today when I looked down at my ring, I noticed it had turned my skin black again. Like me, have you ever wondered why this happens?

Curiosity nudged me to learn that the most common cause is "metallic abrasion" from lotion, of all things. It sounds odd to me that something that makes our hands soft can be abrasive.

Interestingly, skin lotion contains compounds that rub off tiny particles of gold which is a very soft metal. When gold dust is absorbed, it forms a black smudge. Hmm…who knew?

Because 14K gold is 58% pure gold (and 42% other alloys like copper or silver) these alloys can corrode forming dark compounds under moist conditions. Acids from sweat and chlorine from cleaning products can cause alloy corrosion which explains why a dark smudge occurs more often in warm, moist environments.

So if you're like me and you want to avoid the ring around your ring finger, you can avoid hand lotions, abrasive cleaning compounds and sweaty activities while wearing rings.

Choosing a higher karat gold (such as 18K which is 75% gold and 25% alloy) or platinum can also help. But the most ingenious solution is to apply clear nail polish to the inside of your ring to create a barrier. And there you have it—a simple, inexpensive fix in a tiny bottle.[1]

I LIKE UNDERSTANDING WHY SOMETHING HAPPENS AND THEN working toward a solution. How about you? Does solving a problem bring you a sense of accomplishment?

As I look at my wedding ring and think about my marriage, I wish the issues between my husband and me were as easy to solve as the smudge under my ring.

Do you and your spouse (or friends) have misunderstandings…smudges that darken your day? Issues that leave you asking: "Why does it have to be this way?"

Minutes after Dave and I exchanged our wedding vows and the photographer snapped the last picture, we left for our reception. Once in the car Dave looked down at my rings and made a comment that I have remembered for years. He curtly informed me that my wedding band needed to be closest to my heart.

At the altar after he slipped the band on my finger, my engagement ring was closest to my heart. Now he wanted me to switch the placement of the rings on my finger. While I did appreciate and understand **what** he said, I did not appreciate **how** he said it.

It felt abrupt and condescending to me. I felt hurt that he would speak to me, his new bride, in what I perceived to be a harsh, unloving tone. Have you and your husband (or perhaps you and a family member) ever exchanged words that were offered neutrally but were received negatively?

Oh how I wish I could tell you that this was an isolated incident because emotions and stressors were high on our wedding day. I wish I could say that this has not occurred time after time.

Dave often says one thing and I hear quite another. Likewise, during a disagreement he will tell me that it's not **what** I say but it's **how** I say it. Even after years of marriage, we still struggle with communication.

Can you relate? Dave tells me that I take things too seriously always wanting everything to be perfect. I can see his point but also want him to see mine. I want him to speak lovingly. Conversely, he wants me to speak respectfully. While we both agree on the premise, something happens in our humanness. Does this happen to you also?

There are entire books written by marriage counselors on love and respect. I've read dozens and am still no expert. It's two steps forward and one back as I learn from mistakes and from scripture.

It seems to me that *Ephesians 5:21-33 provides a great foundation for relationships:

**"Out of respect for Chris**t,
be courteously reverent to one another."

Paul addresses us ladies first, before he shares with our men. Then in *verses 22-23 he asks us wives to:

"Understand and support your husbands in ways
that show your support for Christ."

Then Paul addresses our husbands saying:

"The husband provides leadership to his wife
the way Christ does to his church,
not by domineering but by cherishing."

So far Paul and I are singing from the same hymnal. I love the word *cherish,* but even more than the word, I love to *feel cherished.* My husband can do this though it doesn't come naturally.

It takes both time and effort.

After a fourteen-hour workday oftentimes Dave is just too tired to make the effort. Maybe your reality is different. If so, know that you've been blessed.

Then in *verse 24 Paul uses a verb that can send us ladies off the high dive, headfirst with a double back flip into the deep end. He says:

> "So just as the church submits to Christ
>     as he exercises such leadership,
>   wives should likewise submit to their husbands."

Hmm...did he just say *submit*? That's not a popular verb among us women. Submitting to Christ, who is perfect and patient, good and gentle, loving and kind is one thing. But submitting to our imperfect husband is harder. Wouldn't you agree?

Just when I'm ready to think that as a single man Paul doesn't understand marriage, he commands our husbands in *verse 25 to:

> "Go all out in your love for your wives,
>     exactly as Christ did for the church—
>   a love marked by giving, not getting."

Husbands are directed to *go all out in love* for us. What Paul is encouraging is balanced, mutual respect and love. That sounds reasonable. Honestly, it sounds lovely, not that it sounds easy.

Since I like to keep things simple, I try to live the golden rule, which tells me to treat others as I would like to be treated (Matthew 7:12a). For years that was my goal with Dave, but I'm not sure I was going about it the right way. I was loving him *like I wanted to be loved*, when he really needed me to respect him like *he needed to be respected*.

I now realize that Dave has very different needs than I do. He desires respect and I crave love. Men and women are empowered so differently.

Recently when Dave and I were on a date, we were in his hybrid Lexis. It was so quiet that it caught my attention. Powered only by electricity as we backed down the driveway, it was silently smooth like a golf cart. I was mesmerized. It felt and sounded so different than my rumbling SUV.

As he accelerated on the highway, gas took over and perfectly delivered the power we needed. Then as we exited the interstate and rolled to a stop, the motor returned to rest; it was inaudible and peaceful. It didn't idle, wasting precious fuel.

And at that moment I was struck by the similarities between my husband and me...and his car. Our marriage is like a hybrid, fueled by electricity and gas. I am fueled by love while David is fueled by respect.

We each have different strengths and weaknesses, yet together we complement each other. Cooperatively we solve problems, just like a hybrid solves both energy and emission problems.

As we pulled away from the stoplight, a light went off in my head. I better understood our differences and needs. Hybrid cars sound and feel so different than traditional cars. Likewise, when words are communicated with love and respect, they sound and feel so different than words communicated without love and respect.

The same words can generate very different results. Now when I think back to my wedding day, I know that Dave didn't mean to hurt me. Like a powerful gas engine, Dave has a powerful voice and a powerful personality.

This power serves a purpose and has its positives, but there are negatives. Likewise, a gas engine is positively powerful, but it can produce harmful emissions that can hurt the environment.

Strong words can hurt. Gas engines idle and idle words can hurt. Dave and I are learning how to work together, complementing each other with love and respect.

Much like hybrid automobiles are more efficient, we have found love and respect allows our communication to be more efficient...with less harmful misunderstandings. The added bonus is that hybrids leave less of a carbon print or residue on our environment, which brings us full circle back to black residues and smudges.

The ugly smudge under my wedding ring from this day forward will remind me that words and deeds–devoid of respect and love–can also leave an ugly residue.

## THE JOURNEY FORWARD:

On our journey forward, when you see a residue around your ring finger, can it prompt you to remember that the men (boys) in your life crave respect and the women (girls) crave love? The *way* we speak–even more than our words–can communicate both respect and love...or the opposite. What is God wanting you to see today about how you communicate with those you love?

# A BUTTERSCOTCH DISK

## AND HOPE

*M*y daughter was choking. Her eyes were as big and as round as the butterscotch disk that was wedged in her windpipe. Though she couldn't speak, she was panicked, begging for help.

That was the longest two minutes my husband and I had ever experienced. It was an otherwise ordinary Sunday. My hubby and son were in the basement watching sports, and Alyssa was coloring at the kitchen table with me writing nearby at my desk.

When I realized what was happening, I spun my daughter around and did the Heimlich maneuver repeatedly. Each time more forceful than the last.

Nothing was working.

I went from being a controlled health care professional to a frantic mom screaming in horror for her husband. Scooping Alyssa up, I ran with her toward the basement.

Dave surged up the stairs, took one look at our little girl and flipped her upside down and started pounding on her back. My David is strong and broad-shouldered. My daughter is delicate and petite. He struck her back with his huge hand…then harder… then harder still…and again. It hurt to watch.

Instinctively I fell to the floor, looking up and cradling her face in my hands. My eyes were locked onto hers. "SHE'S NOT BREATHING!"

And then it was over.

She spoke. Three beautiful words, even more welcomed in that moment than "I love you." Alyssa sputtered, "I swallowed it!" My husband stopped pounding on her back and slowly my heart stopped pounding in my chest. He turned her right side up and gave her a big hug as she recovered, catching her breath.

Now Dave handles emergencies every day as a doctor, but this was his little girl. I could tell he was rattled. And I was completely frazzled. And Alyssa? As she strutted back toward her coloring book, she huffed two final words: "How embarrassing."

Our daughter went without air for a handful of minutes and, just when I thought it was hopeless, against all odds the disk was dislodged and she was free to breathe. Though she rebounded quickly, for days I remembered those manic moments on opposite ends of life's bipolar spectrum.

From hope-starved to hope-filled.

Literally that afternoon they were separated by a single breath. It could have ended so differently. Had my husband been gone, our little girl could've been gone. Short of loading her in the car and racing to the emergency room, I had done everything I knew to do in that moment.

Years later one of my senior high Sunday school students did everything he knew to do. His father choked on a homemade roll during Christmas dinner at his grandma's home. He performed CPR, having been trained as a lifeguard working summers at a local water park. Though ambulances were called, it was too late. His Dad died on the dining room floor that day while his siblings and grandparents watched. Christmas music played in the background. It was surreal.

In the years that followed, a colleague of mine shared her story. Celebrating her husband's thirty-fifth birthday, they had gone out for dinner with friends. When he excused himself from the table abruptly, she didn't think anything of it as the atmosphere was chaotic and festive.

Only when there was commotion near the back hallway leading toward the restrooms did the conversation at the table die down enough for her to hear others relay that a man had choked. Even then she didn't panic, never thinking that it was her strapping hubby.

After a server came to their table with a crazed look on his face, she realized something might be terribly wrong. He led her back to her fallen man, who was now unconscious on the floor. As he laid motionless, an employee administered CPR. Then paramedics loaded him onto a stretcher and she rode with him in the back of the ambulance.

Hope didn't make the trip. That day marked both his birthday–his first day–and his last day.

Life can change as quickly as we can inhale: a butterscotch disk, a yeast roll or a piece of steak. Each can choke hope. Have you ever experienced something that made you feel hopeless? I sure have.

What chokes your hope? Does a death or a diagnosis? Or a disease like diabetes myelitis or malignant melanoma? Failing health or faltering finances can suffocate your hope. Addiction, abuse or abandonment can strangle hope. A spouse being unfaithful can leave us short of breath and short of hope. None of us are immune from being breathless or hopeless. No one.

Hope is like oxygen to our soul. And just as we need oxygen, we need hope to thrive. It's a fact. In medical literature the physi-ological effects of hope are well documented.

Dr. Jerome Groopman is the Chair of Medicine at Harvard Medical School and Chief of Experimental Medicine at Beth Israel Deaconess Medical Center. He's the author of five books and has published 150 scientific articles along with several pieces on hope for *The New York Times* and *The Washington Post*.

In *The Anatomy of Hope*,[1] he explains that researchers are learning that hope has the power to alter neurochemistry. He outlines *belief* and *expectation* as the key elements of hope, saying both can block pain by releasing the brain's endorphins and enkephalins. These mimic the effects of morphine. In some cases hope can also have important effects on respiration, circulation and muscle movement.[2]

Dr. Groopman's research shows that during an illness, hope impacts the nervous system. This starts a cascade, making improvement and recovery more likely. Hope is part of what pharmacists like me have long called "the placebo effect."

Not only for those who are ill but for all of us, hope has a powerful effect on our lives. In a Gallup poll of 1,000,000 people, the *hopeful* said they laughed and smiled much more often than the *hopeless*.[3]

Yet even with all these proven medical benefits of hope, we don't talk about it routinely. We hear sermons preached on faith. We attend classes and study to build our faith.

Meanwhile, books are written on love; we sing about love. Weddings focus on love and rightfully so. The apostle John tells us that God is love (1 John 4:8, 16). In 1 Corinthians 13:13 we learn from Paul that: "three things last forever: faith, hope and love...the greatest of these is love."

When reading this verse I imagine that if hope were personified, she would be the sibling sandwiched between faith and love. Faith would be the big sister, who is known for her leadership. And love would be the little sister, who is the center of attention and steals the show...along with our hearts.

Like a middle child, hope can be overshadowed. Oftentimes hope can be taken for granted, much like air can be taken for granted...until you're choking and have none.

How many books have you read about hope? How many Bible

studies have you attended that focus on hope? How do you even define hope?

Some say that hope is a *wish*. But with faith, we can do so much more than just *wish*. We can have eternal hope. Hebrews 11:1 tells us that "faith shows the reality of what we **hope** for."

The Bible teaches that while faith is built on past experiences, hope is focused on future experiences. Hope oxygenates our souls. Without hope, we're left with a wish. This leaves us breathless, longing for more. A wish is weak, starving for oxygen. With healthy hope we can do more…become more…endure more…and enjoy more!

Would you be surprised to learn that a person can hold their breath nearly twice as long if they inhale pure oxygen before submerging themselves? It's true. The Guinness Book of World Records is 11 minutes 35 seconds for a non-oxygen-aided dive. When given pure oxygen first, the world record is nearly doubled at 24 minutes 3.45 seconds. [4]

Hope, like oxygen, helps us not only survive but to thrive! When we place our hope in God, we learn in Hebrews 6:19:

"This hope is a strong and trustworthy anchor for our souls.
It leads us through the curtain into God's inner sanctuary."

Hope anchors us. It secures us and brings life, leading us into "God's inner sanctuary" right here on earth. Hope isn't meant just for heaven. Hope helps us run the race now.

Sometimes I don't fully appreciate people or things until

they're gone and I can't enjoy them. For me breathing is like that. I don't realize what a blessing it is to breathe freely…until I can't do it. A cruddy cold with congestion helps me appreciate every time I inhale effortlessly.

I find it to be similar with hope. When I'm starved for hope, I know where to go. I swim straight to God. Sometimes I find God in a song on my local Christian radio station, Life 88.5. Oftentimes I find hope in His Word.

Other times I find hope when I take a brisk walk with my thoughts focused on my *Creator*, inhaling fresh air and taking time to notice His *creation*. Many times I find hope in a hug from a friend who cares and will listen.

Amazingly, I've also discovered my hope is replenished when I reach out to others in need. God has a way of returning to us so much more than we give, so much so that our lives overflow with blessings (Luke 6:38).

Practically speaking I have found that when I place my hope in God, I feel happy and secure. When I place my hope in people, I can be disappointed and downcast. Then I find myself hopscotching from one sinking lily pad to another.

May I share a personal example? There have been times when my husband and I have struggled in our marriage. When I focus on Dave, particularly on his imperfections and infractions, I can feel hopeless about our marriage.

I can think: "He's always been this way. This is a part of his personality. He's never going to change. Things are never going to be any different because this is how he's wired. He was raised to respond this way. Life will always be difficult with him."

Did you notice that every sentence is focused on my spouse, not on my Savior? Have you ever found yourself in a similar sinking situation? One where God is sucked right out of the picture?

Like me do you find that you can go from hopeful to hopeless in a matter of minutes? I think this is why we are told to center our thoughts on what is true and honorable, right and pure, lovely and admirable. We are told to think about things that are excellent and worthy of praise (Philippians 4:8). I have this verse beside me as I sit at my desk. The hope we have in Christ oxygenates our souls, so we can soar...and enjoy the simple pleasures in life, like a yummy butterscotch disk.

## THE JOURNEY FORWARD:

On your journey forward, can you put a bag of butterscotch candies on your shopping list? Might you share them with your family and friends, asking them about their greatest hopes? Then together, united in faith, might you pray for those hopes to become reality and write them in your Bible or a prayer journal? Perhaps you can close by surrendering to God in prayer those things that stifle your hope.

# FROZEN

## TWO TRILLION STEPS

*B*urr! It's one degree with a windchill factor of negative twelve degrees. Just like the cover of this book, everything in Kansas City is frozen outside. Meanwhile, I'm warm and toasty inside having just watched the Disney 3D animated movie Frozen.

I love the story of Anna, the fearless princess, who journeys to find Elsa, her estranged sister who has unknowingly frozen the kingdom with her icy magic. As I sit down with a mug of warm cocoa at my computer, I think of another seemingly fearless person who had been frozen for nearly fifty-five years.

Stephen Hawking, an English theoretical physicist and cosmologist, died when he was seventy-six. When he was in his early twenties, Steven was given two years to live when he diagnosed with **Amyotrophic Lateral Sclerosis** (ALS). His ALS was a rare, slow progressing form. Most often ALS or Lou Gehrig's disease "freezes" people within a few years.

Typically the disease appears in those over fifty-five. It only affects nerves that are responsible for the "voluntary" movement of muscles...those that can control our arms and our legs, as well as the muscles involved in speaking and swallowing. The nerves that are "involuntary" are unaffected, so people with ALS still think, see, smell, taste, hear and feel. They are simply frozen. Eventually ALS affects the muscle used for breathing.1

WHILE ALS IS EXTREMELY RARE, BEING FROZEN AT SOME POINT IN life and feeling stuck by overwhelming circumstances is very common.

God's chosen people–the Hebrew nation–were frozen in the desert on a forty-day journey that took forty years. It's a paradox: to be frozen in the desert. Yet in my life, the desert is where I am most prone to freeze.

Do you also find that during dry, dull periods it's hard to move forward? Sometimes during trials, we become frozen and need thawed. Other times, when I've crammed too much in my schedule, I feel deserted and overwhelmed.

Often I want God to magically un-thaw my kingdom, like Princess Elsa and Anna in *Frozen*. At the very least, I reason, He could perform another Jericho miracle with tumbling walls. I sometimes forget what happened before the miracle at Jericho.

Today I reread the account in *Joshua 5:13-14 and found a detail I had forgotten like last week's leftovers in my fridge:

"While Joshua was there near Jericho:
He looked up and saw right in front of him a man standing,
holding his drawn sword. Joshua stepped up to him and said,
'Whose side are you on—ours or our enemies'?"
"He said, 'Neither. I'm commander of God's army.'"

Hmm…I certainly didn't remember this divine encounter. And for heaven's sake, the commander of God's army said he was on "neither" side. I would prefer to have Him loud and proud, cheering me on…thank you very much!

Then we read that Joshua bowed low with his face to the ground worshiping God. He asked for direction in the battle. The Lord's army commander–who we understand to be Christ incarnate–ordered Joshua to remove his sandals, as he was standing on holy ground.

Later in *Joshua 6:3-6 we learn that Jericho's gates were locked, because those inside were fearful of the Israelites. God spoke to Joshua telling him the victory was his:

"Here's what you are to do:
March around the city, all your soldiers.
**Circle the city once. Repeat this for six days.**
Have seven priests carry seven ram's horn trumpets…
**On the seventh day march around the city seven times.**"

After a long blast of the trumpet, the army was to shout, so the walls would collapse, allowing Joshua and his troops to storm the city.

So based on God's instructions (and my math), the army was to circle the city thirteen times. If the city was just one mile from the Israelite camp and it was one mile around the city wall and a mile back to the camp, that's three miles. (Stick with me here.)

Since there is about 2,000 steps per mile each of the 40,000 soldiers walked about 6,000 steps every day for six days. That's 1.4 trillion steps.

The seventh day 40,000 men circled the city seven times (without returning to camp) adding 560,000,000 steps. So this victory was won by over two trillion steps of obedience.

Hmm…and I always thought it was an effortless victory. In fact, I've asked God to "bring walls tumbling down" for myself, my husband and my children. Before I pray that again, I'll remember the **two trillion** steps that were taken obediently in FAITH before the first brick tumbled.

If I were one of those soldiers, I may have thought it made more sense to fight than to circle the city. And while I may have stayed silent, the expression on my face would have said it all. (Really…you've got to be kidding me…march…that's your plan?)

The biggest lesson for me buried in the tumbled walls is to take the first **God-directed** step…then the next…and the next. One step at a time. Trusting. Believing. **Waiting yet walking**!

Whenever I read a Bible story, I ask myself what God wants

me to learn. Can you think of an example from your past where God asked you to step out in faith?

~Maybe you are financially frozen like a fossil in a bad job, frozen with fear about leaving. Yet by faith you stepped out and started a job search. I have experienced this in my career.

~Maybe you are emotionally frozen in unforgiveness because someone in your past has hurt your heart. I have experienced this too.

~Maybe you are physically frozen with poor health. My dad has Parkinson's Disease. His body and mind freeze more and more every day. He struggles to remember the Lord's Prayer each night.

Life isn't as easy or as magical as a Disney movie. COVID quarantines freeze us in our homes. Political polarizations freeze our nation. Racial glaciers freeze our cities. Financial fears freeze us in hard jobs. Emotional hurts freeze our hearts.

But like the Hebrew army lead by Joshua, "In all these things we are more than conquerors through him who loved us (Romans 8:39)." Taking two trillion steps of faith is scary no doubt. Perhaps that's why the most spoken command in the Bible is "fear not." This command appears 365 times. That's once for every day of the year.


THE JOURNEY FORWARD:

What I've found comforting on my journey of a two trillion steps is what Jesus said in Mathew 6:33-34: "Seek the Kingdom of God

above all else, and live righteously, and he will give you everything you need. So, don't worry about tomorrow, for tomorrow
will bring its own worries. Today's trouble is enough for today."
What is God calling you to accomplish today? And will you take
that first God-directed step?

# CAP'N CRUNCH®

## AND CANCER

*A*lyssa's huge hazel eyes looked up at me in shock. She was pinned underneath a 200-pound metal cart filled with groceries on the floor of the cereal aisle at Price Chopper. The front bar of the lower rack awkwardly forced her chin backward. Her sweet, almost-seven-year-old hands gripped the bar that pressed against her windpipe.

It all happened so fast.

One minute she was gazing upward with hope staring at the Cap'n Crunch® and the next minute her little brother came barreling down the aisle full speed. She turned toward him.

BANG.

She was being dragged under the cart like a Swiffer® mop down the aisle all the way past the granola bars. Garrett ran like the wind with his short arms stretched up to reach the handle. He couldn't begin to see over the cart.

He was five and full of boundless energy, finding fun racing the cart like he was in the Indianapolis 500. I chased him screaming. "S-T-O-P-P-P-P-P-P. You've run over your sister!"

An elderly gentleman looked up and stood stunned, holding his box of Grape Nuts®. A stock boy hurried toward me to help, as I instinctively lifted the loaded cart to free my little girl. She was wedged perfectly between the two front wheels. Her chin kept the cart from running over her completely, taking her pudgy little nose off in the process.

I asked the normal mommy questions like, "Are you hurt? Are you sure you're okay?" She had just one question for me. "Mom, just this once could we buy Cap'n Crunch®?" Those big eyes pleaded, beckoning me to say yes. I was so grateful she hadn't been *crunched* that we bought the Cap'n Crunch.

ARE THERE TIMES IN LIFE WHEN ONE MINUTE YOU'RE STANDING upright and the next minute you feel like you've been hit by a cart and pinned to a concrete floor? I've had those days. Recently I had one of those months.

It started when I palpated a lump during a breast self-exam. I'd love to tell you that I was unwavering with my rock-solid faith, but I was scared. My first thoughts were about my little ones.

My husband works crazy-long hours, sometimes fourteen days

in a row when he is on call. Who would read them stories, say prayers and tuck them in bed if something happened to me?

By the end of the week, my gynecologist had worked me in and attempted a needle biopsy. The lump was over a centimeter in diameter, which is large. She couldn't aspirate any fluid, which was a bad sign.

Determining that it was a solid growth, she sent me to the hospital to make an appointment with the interventional radiologist for a biopsy. Weeks after I first discovered the lump, I received the diagnosis of Fibrocystic Breast Disease.

I pulled myself to my feet and praised God that it wasn't cancer. But let me tell you, during the weeks of waiting, I felt dazed…like I was pinned under a grocery cart. Just the thought of cancer is scary.

Maybe you have faced cancer. Perhaps you are battling it right now. Maybe you have a child or spouse who is experiencing medical problems. Or maybe it has nothing to do with health. It might involve lack of finances or lack of faithfulness. Wouldn't it be wonderful if life was simple and a box of Cap'n Crunch could make everything better?

I don't have all the answers, but I do know that during trials, I cling to scripture like my daughter clung to the bottom bar of the cart, just to keep from being run over. I find comfort in verses like 2 Corinthians 4:8-9 where Paul shares:

"We are pressed on every side by troubles,
but we are not crushed.

We are perplexed, but not driven to despair.

We are hunted down, but never abandoned by God.

**We get knocked down, but we are not destroyed."**

I love those pairs: Pressed not crushed. Perplexed not driven to despair. Hunted down but never abandoned. Knocked down but not destroyed.

These promises can provide the encouragement that we need to hang on during trials. I am grateful that these are truths promised by the King of all Kings, not sugar-coated promises made by a fictitious captain on the side of a box of cereal.

When I am in the midst of a trial, God's promises are sustaining. But if I'm totally transparent I admit that I also want a modern-day Barnabas; he was the guy who was nicknamed "Son of Encouragement (Acts 4:36-37)."

He was known for believing the best of people in the worst of circumstances. He was remembered for lifting people up who had been knocked down. What a wonderful testimony.

Who is the Barnabas in your life? If you don't have a Barnabas, maybe you could start praying for one. Please let someone in your church family know of your need.

I have a dear friend who is my encourager. I call her my walking warrior. Each week we meet and walk about five miles in two hours at the mall. With each lap we make, my heart beats faster, but it is lighter. My Barnabas is named Christa Stewart, which is so appropriate because she is *Christ's steward* to me.

We end each walk in the parking lot by our cars in prayer. Life is a bit easier when we have friends to share both the good and the bad. None of us have perfect lives, even though some may look perfect on the outside.

I also find scripture put to music can be encouraging. One of my favorites is *On Eagle's Wings,* based on Isaiah 40:31

> "But those who trust in the Lord will find new strength.
> They will soar high on wings like eagles.
> They will run and not grow weary.
> They will walk and not faint."

Having a Christian radio station may seem like a small thing, but I have found that it can make a **BIG** difference.

What makes a difference in your life? Maybe it's a pet who provides company and comfort. Maybe it's being outside in creation that allows you to most clearly see your Creator. A rainbow can remind us of His promises or a gorgeous sunset can provide a glimpse of God's glory.

He cares for us and He doesn't want us to be pinned down and pulled along by heavy carts. In Matthew 11:28-30 Jesus said:

> "Come to me, all of you who are weary and carry heavy burdens,
> and I will give you rest. Take my yoke upon you.
> Let me teach you, because I am humble and gentle at heart,
> and you will find rest for your souls.
> For my yoke is easy to bear, and the burden I give you is light."

As a working mother of two, I am weary every day. I carry heavy groceries, heavy kids and sometimes heavy burdens. While a one cm lump may weigh less than an ounce, the thought of cancer is heavy.

Jesus offers to teach us, saying that He is humble and gentle. He promises that even when we are tired, we will find rest for our souls. And then He uses an analogy that I know little about. He speaks of yokes.

I have never worn a yoke, nor have I ever used one to force two animals to work together. But I get the gist of what He is promising. When Jesus says that His yoke is easy and His burden is light, I think of my husband as I am "yoked" to him in marriage.

Recently our water heater in the basement went kaput. So we had to haul the old one up the cream-carpeted stairs. My strong husband triple strapped the 300-pound water heater to a dolly and one step at a time hoisted the heater upward.

My job was to follow him up stabilizing the heater if it began to wobble. Dave did all the heavy lifting. I just followed him holding my breath and praying he could make it.

He did. He always does.

My light burden came later as I scrubbed the wet rust marks made by the dripping heater on the carpet. Dave and I are a good team; we always get the job done and I'm grateful for his strength and ingenuity.

Likewise, we are on Christ's team. He offers to help carry one-cm-sized burdens and water-heater-sized burdens. He promises rest for our trapped, sapped souls when life is dreary and we are weary.

### THE JOURNEY FORWARD:

When the kids and I arrived home from Price Chopper, they were so excited. Guess what they wanted to eat for lunch?

As I poured the milk into their bowls, I thanked God that Alyssa wasn't bleeding or bruised and had no broken bones. Then I smiled knowing exactly what I would share with my husband over dinner when he asked about my day.

Now when I grab hold of a handle to push a grocery cart, I thank God for my health and think of someone who has been knocked down and run over by cancer.

Next time you wait in line at the checkout, can you prayerfully ask God to lift a friend's health burdens and send them an encourager? If you don't have an encourager or a church family, maybe you could visit a church you've driven past near your home. You can jump on their website to learn a bit about their fundamental teachings. A Christ-centered church is a blessing!

# THE ISLETS OF LANGERHANS

*I* live in Blue Springs–a suburb on the Missouri side of Kansas City–but I never really knew how the city got its name until recently. When I learned that pioneers named it for the refreshing spring from the Little Blue River, I had to smile.

If we stopped here on our faith expedition, we would find that the river is more like a creek now. While it's near my home, my family enjoys the ocean much more than the creek.

Unfortunately the closest strip of ocean is in Texas, due south beyond the Corpus Christi islets. We often vacationed on the southern shore of Mustang Island. It's a well-kept secret, as it's more of a local hotspot than its neighbor, Padre Island. Seashells and sand dollars along with the rush of waves beckons my family even though it's over fourteen hours from our home.

This brings me to ask, which do you think is closer to KC: Mustang Island or the Islets of Langerhans? Would you be surprised to learn that no matter where you live the Islets of Langerhans are closer than you may think?

The islets aren't anyone's favorite vacation spot as they are found in your pancreas, nestled behind your stomach. Your pancreas and stomach are neighbors. Both are as large as your fist.

We know our stomach well, but how well do we know our pancreas? And how can something like a pancreas point us to God the Father?

Like God the Father, our pancreas protects us. While God has too many jobs to count, our pancreas has two main jobs: one is an outside job (exocrine) and one is an inside job (endocrine).

The exocrine job is to provide enzymes **outside** our pancreas that help metabolize food in our digestive track. The endocrine job is to produce insulin **inside** the pancreas. Insulin is a hormone that regulates blood sugar. The lack of insulin leads to the lack of blood sugar control.[1]

When we think of diabetes, we most often think of Type 2 Adult Onset Diabetes, which affects one in ten Americans. But there's another type of diabetes called Type 1 Juvenile Onset Diabetes, which affects less than one in 200 Americans. It's an autoimmune disease, caused by the immune system attacking the islets that make insulin.[2]

Normally our immune systems protect us much like our earthly fathers protect us. But sometimes both immune systems and fathers are misguided. In this way imperfect fathers mimic imperfect immune systems.

Sometimes dads are damaged from their own childhood and don't break sin's cycle. Some are absent due to work, divorce or bad choices. Some fathers are addicted or abusive. While my dad, Cliff Nale, was loving and kind, I know that some of you may have had dads who were unloving and unkind. To those who had ungodly fathers, I am so sorry.

Throughout this book, I do refer to God as "our Father." This isn't meant to remind anyone of painful memories or associate abusive power with our loving God. There isn't enough space in all the chapters of this book to chronicle the damage done by bad dads.

While this book is not about earthly fathers, it is about our heavenly Father...and He does have something to say about those who harm the innocent. In fact, it's so important that three of the four gospels share His admonition (Matthew 18:6, Mark 9:42, Luke 17:2).

God sent His own Son who had a child sitting on his lap when He gave this warning in Matthew 18:6:

"Anyone who welcomes a little child
like this on my behalf is welcoming me.
But if you cause one of these little ones
who trusts in me to fall into sin,
it would be better for you
to have a large millstone tied around your neck

and be drowned in the depths of the sea."

It was important to Jesus that those who lived through abuse of any kind as a child understand that God doesn't want the innocent to suffer harm. Our earthly fathers are imperfect and love imperfectly. But our heavenly Father is without flaw and loves us flawlessly. His love never fails (Psalm 136:1).

While I was never abused by my earthly father, a dear friend of mine was hurt by her dad again and again while growing up. Her father had a hateful heart; he was controlling and critical, always suspecting the worst.

She still remembers how he would respond to what he considered infractions…how he would barge into her room and conduct searches like the Gestapo. She watched as he controlled her mother and siblings, dictating everything in the home, down to the décor. She promised herself that when she was old enough to leave for college, she would never return to live there.

Amy walked through the shadowy, jagged valleys of her childhood with fear and disdain. Many pages of Amy's story were written first in tears. Undeniably, her father hurt her heart, but she will be the first to tell you that her Creator NEVER left her alone in her pain. Amy shares how God uses everything working it together for her good (Romans 8:28).

Amy put herself through college, without any help from her affluent father. She learned how to survive on day-old bread, making a jar of peanut butter last for weeks. Amy is now a pediatric physical therapist. Daily she helps struggling children. She loves her job despite the avalanche of paperwork and long hours.

Certainly, God uses the good. (Yes, siree. Please give me a double portion of the good!) But God also uses the bad and the ugly, unspeakable things **to bring** good. God does NOT allow the suffering of His children to count for nothing…or to go unnoticed. He sees our tears (Psalm 56:8). He knows of our fears. And He loves us dearly.

Amy is a living, breathing witness that God is faithful in comforting the brokenhearted (Psalm 61:1). Her face glows and her eyes sparkle. She is the first to share that God has given her a "crown of beauty" in exchange for ashes (Psalm 61:3). This imagery breathes hope into my heart. And it makes me smile.

What girl wouldn't want a crown? (I'll leave the scholarly debate over whether these crowns are to be understood literally to those with PhD's in theology and hermeneutics.) Meanwhile, I'll share one of the figurative ways that God has given Amy a "crown of beauty" from ashes.

Like no other friend I have, Amy can readily see good in the midst of bad. She has the God-inspired ability to see diamonds instead of coal.

You may call this a positive outlook. Those health care professionals in her department tell her she has the ability to lead, inspiring others with the power of "positive thinking". Recently during her annual review her boss told her she had "emotional intelligence."

Call it what you want. Amy gives God the glory for her ability to visualize good, when it's invisible to others. Because she has experienced the bad, she also has a greater appreciation for the good. Amy has a heart for those who are hurting. In fact, she has been instrumental in my ministry and even helped me choose the name: Rx For The Soulful Heart.

This Rx brings me back to my training as a pharmacist and to diabetes. In 1922, before insulin, diabetes was a death sentence, taking its victims within two years. By 1926, with insulin, there was a six-fold reduction in death. In 2009, with insulin and other therapies, mortality in Juvenile Onset Diabetes was reduced to only one death per one million.[3] This gives me and those with diabetes true hope!

## THE JOURNEY FORWARD:

As a pharmacist, I can empathize dispensing medications and insulin to patients with diabetes. However, I can't fully stop the immune system from attacking innocent cells, like those Islets of Langerhans. As children of God, we can dispense love in God's name though we can't prevent all abuse.

Today on our journey forward, can you see how God might use the bad you've experienced to bring good to others? You can better relate to those who have similar hurts. Perhaps you could ask God to use the valleys you've experienced to change your perspective. And when someone who hasn't had the protection of a godly father needs your help, will you reach out to them in love?

A BIT MORE INFO AND LOADS OF HOPE FOR THOSE WITH DIABETES: Sugar molecules are ginormous. When they're left floating in the blood, they're like out-of-control semi trucks careening down the "highway" of our blood vessels causing damage. Diabetes is what doctors call a "vascular disease."

They damage all three types of vessels or "highways." Arteries are like interstate highways with fast traffic. Veins are like one-way roads with slow traffic. Capillaries are like side roads in our subdivisions.

As you can imagine, the most damage by these semi truck-size molecules occur in the small vessels. Take a moment to imagine an out-of-control eighteen-wheeler on the side roads in your own neighborhood. It could do major damage careening into kids and cars. That's exactly what happens to different "neighborhoods" or organs in diabetics.

Diabetes causes "end-organ damage" which is the "end result" of too much sugar left to career around in our blood damaging our vessels. In the heart it causes heart attacks. In the brain it causes strokes. In the eyes it causes blindness. Close management allows diabetics to live long lives. Diabetes is no longer a death sentence!

## PLAQUE AND PRIDE

*I*t's the middle of the afternoon and I'm reclining comfortably with my feet up with nothing in the world to do. It's then that I notice how dull the diamond in my wedding ring looks. It seems I have cookie dough from yesterday stuck under the setting.

While my ring may be dirty, my teeth will soon be clean. Oh, did I mention, I'm waiting at my dentist's office for my hygienist to clean my teeth? It's one of the few times moms lay back and lounge in the middle of the day. And it's one of the few times I don't mind waiting.

When my sweet hygienist arrives she flashes me a diamond bright smile and gets started saying… "Open your mouth as wide as you can. Good. Now turn slightly to the left. Terrific. Lower your jaw a bit. Perfect. Stay just as you are."

I attempt to smile back without changing the angle and opening of my mouth. She asks about my children and my day as she smooths the big, blue bib over my blouse and hangs a saliva straw over the rim of my lip.

Next she begins her delicate work scraping hardened plaque from the grooves of my teeth. First one instrument then another. I can taste blood from my gums.

Plaque and tartar takes on a whole new significance. As I lay with my mouth opened and my eyes shut, I wonder about tartar. I knew it wasn't good, but what made it bad?

In short, I learned from my hygienist that enzymes in our saliva accelerate the calcification of plaque into tartar. The areas closest to the saliva ducts have the greatest amount of tartar. Once the plaque is hardened, no amount of diligent brushing can remove it. That's where she helps.

AFTER MY HYGIENIST WAS DONE, WAITING FOR DR. ROSS TO check my mouth, I was left to think. It seems to me that plaque has a lot in common with pride. Let me explain.

If pride is not brushed from our lives, it will harden and adhere. Self-pride and arrogance can erode our life much like plaque and tartar can erode our teeth.

God has as much to say about pride as dentists have to say about plaque. We've all heard that pride comes before the fall. I like how the Message Bible adds "the bigger the ego, the harder the fall" (Proverbs 16:18).

Do you know anyone who thinks they're better than others based on what they have accomplished? If you find this hard to stomach, God does too. In fact we learn that God detests the proud and plans to put the arrogant in their place (*Proverbs 16:5).

Today we don't often label pride for what it is. It's a sin. In fact, God elaborates saying that both arrogance and pride are "distinguishing marks in the wicked" (*Proverbs 21:4). These verses are clear about how God feels about pride, but is all pride bad? Can we be proud of our children when they accomplish their goals? When does pride cross a line and become bad? When accomplishments bring God glory, it's good! We are called to bring God glory (Isaiah 43:7). But therein lies the truth. The glory is for God (Romans 11:36). It's to be given to Him, laid at His feet in thanksgiving.

When pride brings glory to us and we internalize it claiming it as our own, it can harden into arrogance. This is bad like plaque that hardens into tartar. Pride is natural, but it's something we can't let settle on our souls. Similarly, plaque is natural, but we can't let it settle on our teeth.

If we allow our accomplishments to adhere and define us, it's like tartar and can result in decay. Our marriages, our family and our work can all be affected by arrogance. Wouldn't you agree?

So while brushing our teeth is easy, scraping pride from our lives is hard. What are we to do with pride? Paul was once a very proud Pharisee. Then he was literally knocked off his high horse and blinded by a light from heaven.

After three days God restored his sight and Paul never saw life the same way (Acts 9:1-9). He saw through eyes of humility and love. From that day forward, he served others with a grateful heart.

Like an excellent dental hygienist, Paul has some cleansing words of wisdom in Romans 12:1-2:

> "Don't copy the behavior and customs of this world,
>> but let God transform you into a new person
>>> by changing the way you think.
>> Then you will learn to know God's will for you,
>>> which is good and pleasing and perfect."

At work we have regular reviews. We're told to document and share our accomplishments. The world tells us to stand up and speak up...be loud and proud! But God's ways are not the world's ways. God–who sees what we do in private–will reward us (Matthew 6:4).

THE JOURNEY FORWARD:

While brushing your teeth tonight, be reminded to brush pride from your life by giving God **all** the glory for **all** your accomplishments. Though James was no dentist, he understood humility.

He tells us to humble ourselves before God so that He will lift us up (James 4:10).

On our exciting journey forward looking for **Diamonds In Our Days**, let's travel light! Both plaque and pride have no place in our backpacks...or our lives!

# GLUTEN & GRACE

On our faith journey, it's time to pause for a snack. While hiking most folks eat sandwiches, but for some people bread with gluten has got to go! Gluten is a protein in wheat, barley and rye. It causes chaos for thirteen percent of people, who are gluten sensitive or fully gluten intolerant (having Celiac Disease). Because the symptoms of both are very similar, it's difficult to diagnose whether a person has Celiac Disease or is simply gluten sensitive.

Celiac Disease is a chronic inherited disease. When exposed to gluten, the immune system produces an antibody that attacks the lining of the small intestine. The result is the villi (which normally look like blades of grass) on the bowel wall look like they've been "mowed down". These shorter "blades of grass" are less able to absorb nutrients. This can lead to malnutrition, anemia, osteoporosis and possibly increases in certain types of cancer.[1]

TODAY WE HEAR A LOT ABOUT GLUTEN INTOLERANCE IN THE media. We also hear a lot about general intolerance in the media. People can be polarized and pitted against each other. Christians can be intolerant of Muslims. Whites can be intolerant of blacks. Democrats can be intolerant of Republicans.

In God's Word we see lots of examples of intolerance. Jews (the chosen people) were intolerant of Gentiles (non-Jews). Sadducees (aristocratic Jewish leaders who did not believe in life after death) were intolerant of the Pharisees (middle-class Jewish leaders who did believe in life after death). Clean (healthy) people were intolerant of unclean (unhealthy) people. Jews (pure-breeds) were intolerant of Samaritans (half-breeds).

Roman citizens (privileged) were intolerant of non-Romans (unprivileged). Men (stronger) were intolerant of women (weaker), who had few rights. Free men were intolerant of slaves. As many as one in three of the population in Rome and one in five across the Roman Empire, were slaves.[2]

Even within the Temple there were very strict lines drawn. These lines dictated where you were allowed and where you were *not* allowed (Stick with me here as we carefully tiptoe forward.).

The very most outer court was the Court of Gentiles, followed by a second outer Court of Women. Then the Court of Israel–

which was only for men. Next was the Holy Place, which was only for Levitical priests. Finally was the Holy of Holies. Only once a year did one priest enter on the Day of Atonement (known as Yom Kippur).

The very moment Jesus died, God made a statement about tolerance for ALL humankind to see. We can read about it in Matthew 27:50-51:

> "Then Jesus shouted out again, and he released his spirit.
> **At that moment the curtain in the sanctuary of the Temple**
> **was torn in two, from top to bottom.**"

Being torn from the top down indicated that God Himself split the curtain that separated Him from all humankind.

In the moment Jesus gave up His Spirit dying for our sins, God received His sacrificial death for the atonement of **ALL** our sins. Anyone can come to Him through faith in Jesus. Muslims and Christians. Republicans and Democrats. Blacks and whites. Women and men. Gentiles and Jews. Unhealthy and healthy. Poor and rich. Uneducated and educated.

In God's eyes ALL of us are extended the grace of salvation! God draws a circle that includes everyone. Which brings us full circle back to intolerance, specifically dietary intolerances.

I find it telling that we even divide gluten intolerance into two types: Celiac and Non-Celiac. Both have the same symptoms. Yet even the symptoms we divide into two groups: G.I. (gastrointestinal upset) and non-G.I. (headache, fogginess). Yet both have the same treatment–a gluten-free diet.

Likewise, we may not all have the same religious belief, political affiliation, skin color, status, gender, education, nationality or language, but we all have the same need. We each need the Savior!

Christ speaks the language of grace and love…not exclusion and intolerance. In Romans 14:1-3 we're encouraged to welcome others with open arms even if they don't see things the way we do. We're told not to jump all over them every time they do or say something with which we disagree. Even when they are:

> "strong on opinions but weak in the faith department.
> Remember, they have their own history to deal with.
> **Treat them gently."**

Then the apostle shares that a person who has walked in their faith for many years may be comfortable eating and drinking both kosher and non-kosher foods. There may be others who are new to their faith, who assume they should be a vegetarian and eat accordingly.

While this may sound unimportant to us, it was extremely important in the early church because Jewish laws had prohibited them from eating with Gentiles due to their dietary restrictions. As Christians, God wanted them to be able to sit down together as one church.

Since we all are guests at God's table, we are told it would be rude if we criticized each other about what we ate or didn't eat. After all, Christ invited us each to the table. Paul reminds us that we don't have any business crossing people off the guest list or interfering with God's welcome. If there are corrections to be made or manners to be learned, God can handle that without our help (Romans 14:4).

Even today we sometimes forget that we're called to reach out to others in love, leaving the judgment and resulting punishment to God (Matthew 7:1). This brings us full circle to a quote I love. Billy Graham said:

> "It is the Holy Spirit's job to convict,
> God's job to judge and
> **my job to love**."

THE JOURNEY FORWARD:

While the treatment for gluten intolerance is a **gluten-free** diet, the solution for general intolerance is **free grace** through Christ (Ephesians 2:8).

On our journey forward today, will you reach out to someone you might otherwise not tolerate or associate with and share a smile, a kind word or maybe even a coffee?

# TRANSIENT ISCHEMIC ATTACKS

## AND TRANSIENT VERBAL ATTACKS

*T*ransient Ischemic Attacks (TIA)are sometimes called "mini strokes." They don't last long and most people recover fully. As you might suspect, they're more common in older folks and are often a warning sign for a full-blown stroke.

Both TIA's and strokes have similar symptoms, like blurred vision, numbness, weakness and even temporary paralysis. Oftentimes, people can't speak to tell you what they are experiencing.

So what can we do if we think someone is having a stroke? If they haven't had any head trauma that may have caused bleeding in their brain, pharmacists suggest taking an aspirin immediately. To help the aspirin dissolve, have them chew it followed by a warm glass of water. Next call 911 or rush them to the hospital. While aspirin is a weak "blood thinner," the emergency room has faster, stronger "clot busters" that can be lifesaving.[1]

TODAY I WAS SPEAKING TO A DEAR FRIEND FROM CHURCH WHO recently experienced a Transient Ischemic Attack. Having attended many of my classes, she has shared her testimony over the years. She was a victim of verbal abuse by her first husband who left her alone to raise their children.

Knowing her story as I spoke with her, I was struck by how much "Transient Ischemic Attacks" have much in common with "Transient Verbal Attacks." Like TIA's, Transient Verbal Attacks leave us numb and paralyzed like a stroke. They can result in weakness and can "blur our vision" on life. Just as multiple mini strokes can be cumulative and devastating, wounding words can be cumulative and devastating.

We've all heard the nursery rhyme: "Sticks and stones may break my bones, but words will never hurt me." While this may rhyme, making it easy to repeat and remember, it isn't true. Words do wound. *Proverbs 12:18 tells us:

> "Rash language cuts and maims,
> but there is healing in the words of the wise."

I have a second closer friend whose husband carelessly used demeaning profanity, calling her names when he was irritated, tired or angry. The words were spoken in the privacy of their home. Since others didn't see his hurtful behavior, he wasn't willing to acknowledge the abuse. Like Transient Ischemic

Attacks, after the episode had ended, there were no visible findings. But make no mistake, these "Transient Verbal Attacks" did occur and did hurt her heart.

Amanda would share her pain when we met privately over coffee. Tears would flow as we talked. Through it all, she loved her husband, never returning his profanity.

While I was no expert in psychology, I could listen and empathize. For years Amanda didn't want to admit that what she was experiencing was in fact verbal abuse. I sensed that naming it made it too real.

Amanda and I both were Christian women who longed for marriages that honored God. Because she wasn't being physically abused and the attacks did not directly involve her children, she made the decision to keep her family intact.

Honestly, I struggled seeing her in pain. Some weeks were fairly normal; but during those difficult weeks, she needed a friend who would pray with her.

If you're experiencing verbal abuse, do you have someone with whom you can meet regularly? None of us have lives that are perfect. If we could script our own stories, we would choose to leave out certain chapters. For those difficult pages, friends can be a blessing.

While Amanda always knew she didn't deserve to be cursed, her husband always found ways to blame her. Trying to make peace with him, she was prayerful. Each week we would pray for our husbands, our children and their faith journey.

Through pain our hearts were knit together, like carbon atoms bond under pressure forming strong diamonds. As years became decades, we could see the results of our prayer. Slowly, Amanda's husband began to soften. The "Transient Verbal Attacks" occurred less frequently.

Together we turned fifty and Amanda began to wisely hold her husband accountable. While he still spoke harshly at times, profanity and name calling were no longer his primary response.

While some weeks were still frustrating, Amanda could see that her husband had made progress...even if it was two-steps-forward-one-step-back, imperfect progress.

God can supernaturally strengthen us through Biblical friendships. In scripture we are encouraged to help those in need and share their burdens (Galatians 6:2). Like diamonds, we can reflect light and brighten the days of those who are struggling.

From the outside, my friend looked like she had a charming life. The mother of three healthy boys, she was always creatively decorating her sweet country cottage. She had a high-paying job and the perfectly petite figure. She was a strong woman of faith... yet she was abused.

While the intensity, type, frequency and duration of abuse varies greatly, all abuse hurts. Most people have experienced verbal abuse at some point in life.[2] Perhaps our abuser was a grade school bully, a micromanaging boss, an overbearing father, a manic mother, an alcoholic spouse, boyfriend or sibling.

Like strokes, verbal abuse comes from different sources and may present differently, but the result can be crippling. Jesus doesn't mince His words when He warns and informs us in Matthew 12:36:

> "And I tell you this,
> you must give an account on judgment day
> for every idle word you speak."

I could see how words bruised Amanda's heart. If you're the victim of "Transient Verbal Attacks," you too know how hearts are hurt by words.

## THE JOURNEY FORWARD:

There are people all around us who ache. On our journey forward, might God be able to use your hurt to help others? In this way God could beautifully bring good from the bad you have suffered (Romans 8:28). Can you use your words to support, encourage and embolden those you love? Can you be the **Diamond in their Day**?

# RESTLESS LEGS

## AND RESTLESS MINDS

*O*n our faith journey we each have difficult challenges. I have a heart for people who struggle with Restless Legs Syndrome. Some nights when I lay down at night to sleep, my brain keeps misfiring, sending my legs the message to move and twitch, even though I'm desperately trying to stay still. It's like feeling an itch that you tell yourself you shouldn't scratch. Meanwhile the itch becomes more intense, begging you to give in and scrape.

Symptoms of Restless Legs Syndrome are relieved by moving. So when it was time to buy a new mattress, my husband and I replaced our box spring mattress with a foam mattress so my movement wouldn't radiate through the mattress waking him.

WHILE RESTLESS *LEGS* SYNDROME AFFECTS ROUGHLY 33 MILLION Americans,[1] what I call Restless *Mind* Syndrome affects countless more. Do you ever lay down at night to sleep, but your mind won't turn off? Do your thoughts ever ruminate with worry as you chew on "what ifs"?

Worry leads to restlessness and has robbed me of countless hours of sleep. As a woman of faith, I know God wants me to trust Him. During the day when it's light, I do better walking by faith. But during the night when it's dark, my thoughts can be overpowered as my brain is naturally wired to worry.

Did you know that as women, our brains are wired differently than men's brains? We have more connective tissue or gray matter in our brains. While this allows us to focus on multiple things at once (a baby crying while simultaneously cooking dinner and listening for the washer spin cycle to stop), it also makes it harder to disconnect and "power down" at night to reboot.[2] Women thus can be more prone to think about multiple things and worry.

Now I know what the Bible has to say about worry from verses like *Philippians 4:6-7 where I'm told:

> "Don't fret or worry. Instead of worrying, pray.
> **Let petitions and praises shape your worries into prayers,**
> letting God know your concerns.
> Before you know it, a sense of God's wholeness,
> everything coming together for good,
> will come and settle you down. It's wonderful what happens
> when Christ displaces worry at the center of your life."

Most nights I pray myself to sleep. But some nights worry still seeps in like a stealth software virus that won't let my system power down.

On those nights–even though I desperately need sleep–I slip out of bed and move. I close the bedroom door behind me. Then I walk and talk to God. Sometimes I sing hymns, so it's probably a good thing that no one is awake to hear me; no one but my Creator appreciates me a cappella.

Even though I'm moving, my soul is still. Even though I'm noisy, my heart is quiet. And even though I'm moving, I am at rest. So maybe my *restless* legs, with God's help, bring *rest* to my heart.

I'll be the first to say I would rather be like my husband and fall asleep effortlessly, but God has His ways. I know He has my best interests at heart (Jeremiah 29:11). And though I'm sleepy and my vision is blurry, my spiritual vision is Windex® clear as I read the promise of 2 Corinthians 4:17-18 which reminds me:

"For our present troubles are small and won't last very long.
Yet they produce for us a glory that vastly outweighs them
and will last forever!
So we don't look at the troubles we can see now;
rather, we fix our gaze on things that cannot be seen.
For the things we see now will soon be gone,
but the things we cannot see will last forever."

When I do finally return to bed, I don't count sheep but rather

I count my blessings. God knows I have so much to learn that sometimes He chooses to teach me late into the night!

Sometimes lessons come during the day from unlikely places. Recently while at a cooperate meeting, my boss shared a TED talk by Tim Harford. Dr. Harford gave multiple examples of how annoying challenges can either derail you or can make you stronger. He shared a study done by a psychologist named Daniel Oppenheimer.

Dr. Oppenheimer asked high school teachers to reformat the handouts that they were giving to some of their classes. While half of the students would be given handouts that were formatted in something straightforward like Times New Roman, *others would be given more complex fonts like Comic Sans italicized that were difficult to read.*

*At the end of the semester the students who'd been asked to read the more difficult fonts scored better on exams. WHILE THE DIFFICULT FONT HAD SLOWED THEM DOWN, IT FORCED THEM TO WORK HARDER AND THINK MORE ABOUT WHAT THEY WERE READING. They learned more and they grew. I trust that God can use challenges-like restless legs and funky fonts-to help you and me grow.*

## THE JOURNEY FORWARD:

God uses the hard to form beauty. This is the lesson we are learning from the diamond. While you may not know the frustration of Restless Legs Syndrome, might you have annoyances like worry that make you restless? If you're not wired to worry, might you have aches and pains that disrupt your plans?

On our journey forward, what blessings might be disguised as irritations and what lessons might be learned by these annoyances? These are questions I ask myself when everyone else is sleeping. And no matter how difficult or worrisome the day or night, I remind myself of something Billy Graham often said that comforts me: "I've read the last page of the Bible, it's all going to turn out all right."

# FAMOUS COUPLES

here's Prince Charles and Diana. Prince William and Kate. And Prince Harry and Meghan. Each are famous couples. While fame and royalty grab our attention, it fades over time. This leads me to ask: in thousands of years, do you think these couples will still be remembered?

When I think of famous couples, I don't think of royalty and wealth, rather I think of the most famous Book ever written spanning over 4,000 years. Chronologically, I think first of Abraham and Sarah.

The next power couple is Isaac and Rebekah. They had a unique love story that started off great but hit the rocks when life wore on.

Then there's the third generation of patriarchs. Like their parents, Jacob and Rachel were deeply in love and committed to one another. Yet, they too suffered setbacks.

These first three couples in the line of patriarchs each shared a specific heartbreaking trial. Add to these three well-known couples three more pairs, who had famous children.

We know the story of strong Samson (the gullible guy who fell head over heels in love with deceitful Delilah). But have we've forgotten the story about his folks?

Similarly, we remember wise Samuel, the most well-known and well-loved judge over Israel who anointed both King Saul and then King David. Again we often forget about his parents (Elkanah and Hannah).

While we certainly remember John the Baptist, the cousin and forerunner of Christ, we sometimes forget his dad and mom (Zechariah and Elizabeth). Might you guess what grief was shared by all six of these couples?

Each experienced the heartbreak of barrenness for a time. We don't need to look far to find couples who struggle with infertility. They may be our neighbor. Or they may sit in the church pew in front of us.

Each Sunday my family sits behind Noah and Ella. They are gentle souls who have been married for seven years. Both have hearts that hurt. Last year, they lost three children. Two died before they were ever able to hold them. Then baby Joseph arrived two months early. Ella held Joseph's tiny corpse. He never took his first breath or his last breath.

Birth and burial shouldn't be separated by a single day. Such hope and excitement swallowed by such sorrow. This kind, young couple shares the excruciating loneliness of infertility with nearly

50,000,000 other couples. Reproductive endocrinologists tell us there are many reasons for the barrenness; some are treatable.

Statistics speak volumes of grief written in tears. About five percent of couples are never able to have their own biological children. Twelve to eighteen percent experience infertility for at least one year. While no one is to blame, half the time infertility is linked to men and the other half to women. In twenty-five to fifty percent of cases it's a combination of both.[1]

WHILE NEARLY 4,000 YEARS SEPARATE THE PATRIARCHS FROM Noah and Ella at my church, their stories are linked by the pain of infertility. Barrenness and birth seem an eternity apart on the bipolar spectrum of life. For some, conceiving is effortless but for others, barrenness is their burden. While you may not be one of the nearly 100 million individuals who have struggled to conceive, you may struggle with periods of barrenness, loneliness and loss.

Is there something today that makes your world seem barren? So many people suffer from periodic or ongoing loneliness. We each experience ups and downs. You and I teeter and totter between joy and sorrow.

The natural response to loss is sadness. Loss is raw and real. Mourning cannot be hurried or buried alive. What has been your greatest loss? The death of a child—even if the child is older—is excruciating. Perhaps the death of a spouse has brought agonizing isolation. The death of a marriage is the painful death of dreams of what was once promised "until death do us part." What are we to do with dead dreams? How do we bury the hope of what will never be?

No matter what season of barrenness you might be facing, God is with you. He wants to walk with you so you can be strong and courageous when you feel weak and afraid. He promises to never leave or forget you (Deuteronomy 31:6). God shares in detail the struggles of barren people in the Bible so that we can be encouraged by their stories. They aren't fairy tales of lives perfectly lived. Oh no. These are biographies of everyday messed up lives, lies and multiple wives consumed and consummated with jealousy and rivalries. Many passages are rated R.

Abraham and Sarah shouldered nearly seventy-five years of barrenness. We can read about the not-so-faith-filled founding father when he laughed to himself in disbelief. He thinks out load in Genesis 17:17:

"How could I become a father at the age of 100?
And how can Sarah have a baby when she is ninety years old?"

I'm so glad God included the disbelief of our patriarchs instead of painting a perfect picture that would've been flawless but fake. This famous couple struggled to believe they would have one child...never mind entire nations of descendants that would include royalty.

Looking for the happy, sappy ending, I often jump over the

yucky, mucky details. Sarah became so desperate for a baby, she laid her marriage on the altar of adultery and asked her husband to impregnate her servant girl. Imagine how hard it was for ninety-year-old, heartbroken, sagging Sarah to hope? God gets real with us, entrusting us with the raw, imperfect details. Ultimately, Abraham and Sarah do conceive. When their long-awaited child arrives, they name him Isaac, meaning in Hebrew "he will laugh" (Genesis 21:6).

When a trial is over, it's easier to laugh...but during the trial, it's hard to find humor! Have there been times when people look at your life and think it's pretty perfect, but you know better? It's likely there have been times that it's easier to pretend things are okay than to share the ugliness of your reality.

We each struggle with barren valleys. Sometimes they resurface again and again and even afflict our children. This was the case for Abraham and Sarah's infertility. It ran in the family. When their son Isaac and Rebekah were struggling to conceive, I wonder if they ever went to their folks to share their sorrows.

We read about Isaac and Rebekah and their battle against barrenness in Genesis 25:21:

> "Isaac prayed hard to God for his wife
> because she was barren.
> God answered his prayer and Rebekah became pregnant."

One sentence with twenty words spanned nearly twenty years

of infertility. We learn that Isaac was forty when he got married and sixty when he became a dad (Genesis 25:20, 26).

As women we understand the flow of our cycles. Rebekah had twelve periods every year for twenty years. That's 240 times she bled as her heart bled. God said "not yet," but it likely sounded like NO.

Rebekah was now middle-aged. Thankfully, Isaac had learned from his parents not to use the accepted fertility methods of the day. There were no sperm banks, artificial insemination clinics or test-tube babies, but Isaac didn't turn to a younger woman. Instead he turned to God in prayer. God honored his faithfulness and gave him a double portion. Quite literally, Isaac became a dad doubly blessed with twin boys—Jacob and Esau.

Fast forward and infertility strikes again in the third generation of this famous family. Jacob struggled with infertility with the love-of-his-life, Rachel. Unfortunately, when Rachel was desperate, she turned to the world instead of turning to God. Rachel fell into the same trap as her grandmother. Like Sarah, Rachel thought God needed help and arranged for her hubby to sleep with her servant to bear sons on her behalf.

After "many years" of barrenness and much stress on the marriage, Rachel gave birth to a son and named him Joseph (Genesis 30:22). Tragically, Rachel died while giving birth to their second son, Benjamin (Genesis 35:18). In total, Jacob had four wives and twelve sons—resulting in the twelve tribes of Israel. I can summarize their story in this one simple paragraph, but I can't imagine living the complex, everyday trauma of four wives in a race to procreate.

I believe God shares these struggles with barrenness so that when we struggle we can learn from both their faithful and their faithless failures. When we go to God in prayer, covenants are fulfilled. When we run to the world, we weave webs.

God didn't stop with the infertility stories of the first three generations of our faith family. He tells us about Samson's parents' struggle with infertility (Judges 13:2). Samson's story is riddled with both stupidity and strength, the latter of which he used to deliver Israel during the twenty years he was judge.

Unlike Samson, Samuel was wise; he was the greatest and last judge. His parents were Elkanah and Hannah. When Hannah was unable to conceive, Elkanah took a second wife (Peninah) who was cruel to Hannah, taunting her. Rather than turn on her husband, Hannah turned to God in prayer for years and in due time she gave birth to a son. She named him Samuel, proclaiming, "I asked the Lord for him" (1 Samuel 1:20).

Never knowing if Samuel would be her one and only child, we read that when he was weaned she took him to the Temple to fulfill her promise to give him to God (1 Samuel 1:28). God is gracious to share that Hannah was blessed with three more sons and two daughters. (He also knows that we women like happy details.)

Like Samson and Samuel, John the Baptist was also a long-awaited answer to prayer for his folks—Zechariah and Elizabeth —who were both old. Sometimes God answers prayer in such a way that we know it was Him because it's otherwise impossible. Zechariah knew it was inconceivable for Elizabeth to have a child naturally. This was a supernatural birth confirming that with God all things are possible!

These six couples shared a similar heartbreak. Unlike today, in Biblical times barrenness was not medically understood and the woman was sadly blamed and shamed. Today we know from testing that both men and women can have infertility issues. I'm grateful that as women, we live in an age where we are valued for more than just our ability to procreate. Both women who have children and those who do not are of equal importance in God's eyes! Together, we are valued as much as men by our Creator.

Why do I spend the time to highlight six of the many couples of the Bible who struggled with barrenness? Because when we read about God's faithfulness, we can be encouraged when we're swallowed with sadness. There are times when I'm in the midst of trials where, if I could just see through to the other side, I could be renewed.

## THE JOURNEY FORWARD:

When we hear the names of Isaac, Jacob, Joseph, Samson, Samuel and John we think of the great men...often forgetting their parents' struggle with infertility. Why? So often when prayers have been answered, we forget the anguish of the trial. These boys are all an answer to prayer and stand as living testimonies to God's faithfulness!

When we turn to God, He can work all things together for our good just as He has done for the sweet couple who sits in front of my family at church each Sunday. Recently Ella gave birth to Lydia. Today she was baptized into God's eternal family. Rejoice with this precious family and give God the glory for baby Lydia's miraculous birth.

# AGONISTS AND ANALOGS

*P*eanut butter and jelly. Cowboys and Indians. Agonists and analogs. We all know about the first two pairs, but agonists and analogs are allusive...unless you spend a lot of time in a pharmacy like I do. Agonist and analogs are two of the most common types of pain medicines.

A drug that is an agonist stimulates a receptor. An example is morphine for pain relief. A drug that is an analog looks very similar to a molecule the body makes itself. An example is opioids for pain relief. The analog is mistaken for the true McCoy and the body is "duped" into a particular mode of action.

Biochemist have learned how to make analogs that mimic our bodies natural agonists providing relief for everything from cancer pain to Parkinson's Disease. In the medical realm, this is good. But the line between relief and abuse can be blurred.

Although the opioid crisis is relatively new, the problem between good and evil has existed since Lucifer rebelled against God and was cast out of heaven. I understand that some Bible scholars believe that this is a story to explain the beginning of evil in our world. I'll leave the debate to those with much higher and holier degrees. What there is no doubt about is that Jesus is the Light of the World (John 8:12).

Lucifer is a thief. He comes to steal and kill and destroy. Jesus tells us that He comes to give us a rich and satisfying life (John 10:8-10). I believe this with all my heart.

Sometimes we want life's decisions to be as easy to make as the black print on this white page is to read. No one would ever choose a life of addiction losing everyone and everything they hold dear dying an early, lonely death. But the first step towards addiction is sometimes blurred. It appears less foreboding...even enticing.

Lucifer himself was described as beautiful Light Bringer. This seems good. As the light bringer, Lucifer can cast confusing shadows so that we doubt God and ourselves. Lucifer blurs the lines between good and evil with these shifting shadows.

Like Eve, you may become confused because Lucifer makes evil look good. When we look back, hindsight makes Eve choice seem short-sighted and silly. As I look back on some of the decision's I made in my life, they too have been short-sighted and silly.

Eve looked at the fruit and "saw that it was pleasing to the eye (Genesis 3:6)." My first love was pleasing to the eye. All the girls wanted to be noticed by him. He was handsome and hunky…and he had dimples when he smiled that melted my heart.

I knew Shawn was not serious about his faith. I also knew God's one instruction to me concerning who I should date and ultimately marry. I was to choose a believer with whom I was equally yoked (2 Corinthians 6:14). God kept His instruction simple. CHOOSE A BELIEVER.

All other choices were mine. I could choose a tall, dark and handsome guy or a blonde haired, blue eyed, bulky, brilliant believer (that's who I ultimately chose).

Unlike many parents, God is silent when it comes to the profession of our spouse. He doesn't favor a doctor or a lawyer over a bookkeeper or street sweeper (my dad was the latter).

Introvert or extrovert.

Athletic or nerdy.

Red-neck and rugged or

Stiff-necked and stubborn.

The choice is all ours. Literally, we each have a free will and can choose from the billions of options world-wide. But the one thing God advises is for us CHOOSE A BELIEVER.

Likewise, Eve (and Adam) could choose to eat of any tree in the garden. ANY EXCEPT ONE. God's one instruction was to NOT eat the forbidden fruit of the tree of the knowledge of good and evil. God didn't have a long list. He kept it simple…avoid the tree in the middle.

Much like Eve, I ignored God's short list. I choose my will over His wisdom.

My first love ended tragically. This hunky, handsome, muscle-bound, dimple bearing pharmacy student broke my heart. I knew God wanted better for me, but all I wanted was Shawn. Know the feeling? Our desires can deceive us. Perhaps that's why we are told to delight in God so He can give us the right desires (Psalm 37:4).

Now years later, I am so grateful that Shawn broke up with me for another girl. While it broke my heart at the time, I can now see that this was a blessing. Although Shawn did graduate from pharmacy school, he has been on probation for substance abuse through the years. He continues to violate probation and his name appears in publications by the state board of pharmacy. Never in a million years would I have guessed that addition was in his future.

I was in love with Shawn. But the high's were followed by incredible lows. Like Eve, I let my eyes and my heart lead me. I choose the ONE THING that God had warned me to avoid. In the Garden of Eden we read that the serpent was shrewd and he came with a seemingly harmless question. "Really, did God say you must not eat the fruit from any of the trees in the garden (Genesis 3:1)?" Lucifer wanted Eve to doubt herself and God. But instead of turning to walk away…Eve entertained evil and answered. She explained that "Of course they could eat fruit from the trees in the garden just not the fruit from the tree in the middle of the garden."

Up until this point…she had it right. Then she got one itsy-bitsy detail wrong. She quoted God as saying, "'You must not eat it **or even touch it**; if you do, you will die.'"

Now this snake had his proverbial "foot in the door." God never said a thing about not touching it. God said don't eat it. Eve added the "don't touch it" rule.

The snake informed Eve that she wouldn't die, but rather he explained that "God knows that your eyes will be opened as soon as you eat it, and you will be like God, knowing both good and evil (Genesis 3:5)."

Actually, that was partially true. Eve's eyes would be open and she would be like God knowing both good and evil. Being like God is good. We are called to be like God as we live out our faith. Lucifer enticed Eve with good. Knowing good from evil is a good thing.

The problem then and now is when we disobey God. Disobedience is never rewarded. Even when the thing we want to accomplish is good, the mean doesn't justify the end.

The devil is in the details and he doesn't play fair. He inserted question marks where God had placed periods. Eve "saw that the tree was beautiful and its fruit looked delicious, and she wanted the wisdom it would give her. So she took some of the fruit (Genesis 3:6)."

Did you catch that...Eve touched the fruit. She had it in her hand before she took the first bite. And...she didn't die. Then we read that "she ate it and gave some to her husband, who was with her, and he ate it, too. At that moment their eyes were opened, and they suddenly felt shame at their nakedness (Genesis 3:6)."

Eve didn't die when she touched it...so she went one step further down the path. That's exactly what I did. Shawn first asked me to the Fall formal and I reasoned. He's the cutest guy on campus...and I don't have a date...I really want to go. What harm is one date.

For Eve and Adam, the results of their sin were immediately realized. You and I have been trying to cover our sin ever since. Eve and Adam sewed fig leaves together to make clothes. But imagine how quickly these leaves would dry up and crack exposing them. And imagine how scratchy these dried leaves would be. It was God who made clothes for them out of the animal skins.

We don't know if it was a lamb that was slaughtered to cover them. If it was it would point toward the spotless Lamb of God who would one day cover their nakedness and sin. Whatever the animal, Eve and Adams sin led to the death of an innocent creature. Their sin also led to the death of their innocence.

Shame feels awful. I know. I wore shame during the time I dated Shawn. While I never fully gave myself to him physically, the lines between black and white where blurred to a guilty gray.

I was in love. Shawn was in lust. Have there ever been times in your life when you have confused the two? Love is good and we are told that love is eternal (1 Corinthians 13:13). Lust is cheap, a counterfeit that can be mistaken for love. Lust lasts just a few semesters. I learned the hard way.

THE JOURNEY FORWARD:

Lucifer loves to steal (our dreams), kill (our faith) and destroy (our lives). In short, he loves to break our hearts. He is called the deceiver for a reason. So the next time he comes masquerading as an angel of light (2 Corinthians 11:14) turn to the true Light-Jesus-not a phony analog.

# TORSADE DE POINTES

*A*s we mine for **Diamonds In Our Days**, Torsade de Pointes may sound like a jeweler's most exquisite marquise but it's not.

Torsade De Pointes is a deadly heart rhythm. A French cardiologist named it "Twisting of the Points" because the points of the EKG look twisted. Thankfully, Torsade is uncommon.

While I studied it in pharmacy school, I had never encountered it. That changed the day my husband and I brought our daughter home from the hospital after a prolonged, intense labor. Nurses came running to find my husband, an internal medicine doctor. In the labor and delivery waiting room, a man who had just become a grandfather tumbled out of his chair, clutching his chest.

When the family summoned the nurses, their father was not breathing. When nurses summoned Dave, he immediately started

CPR. Dave asked the charge nurse to find what's called a "crash cart" so he would have with lifesaving equipment and drugs. A code blue was announced overhead, bringing a surge of other healthcare professionals.

My husband placed the cardioversion paddles on this man's chest to jump start his heart. That's when Dave diagnosed Torsade de Pointes.

Dave delivered 200 joules of electrical current with no change in the heart rhythm. So he administered a second massive jolt of electricity.

The man's family was stunned. As if they too had been shocked by electricity, they were silent and still...and then they heard it. The beep of the EKG machine signaled a newly beating heart.

A new birth and a near death all within moments.

To stabilize the new grandfather, Dave started an I.V. and prepared him for transport from the maternity unit to the cardiac care unit. Had the gentleman coded five minutes later Dave and I would have been gone...and the outcome may have been very different.

As I reflect on that day, I am grateful for my daughter's new life and for this grandfather's new lease on life. Golly, it could have ended so differently. When I think of how deadly

Torsade de Pointes can be, I see how much it has in common with legalism.

Legalism is the teaching that God requires more than faith to be saved. Both Torsades and legalism are terminal. One results in cardiac death, while the other results in spiritual death. Legalism twists the whole point of Jesus's death. We are saved by grace through faith in Him, not by our own good works (Ephesians 2:8-9).

Like a cardiologist (who has thirteen years of formal training beyond high school) Paul had years of formal training in the Jewish law. We learn that Paul studied under Gamaliel (a famous Jewish Rabbi) who was known for his Godly wisdom. Yet in all this training, Paul keeps things simple in Romans 3:28:

> "So we are made right with God through faith
> and not by obeying the law."

Just as a physician who acts quickly when they see a patient in Torsade, Paul acted quickly when he saw legalism. He made sure people understood that we can't save ourselves with our good works. We need Jesus.

Before Luke wrote the gospel bearing his name, he was known as Dr. Luke. In Luke 11:38-52 he gives us a very detailed account of how Jesus dealt with legalism during his ministry.

When Jesus was invited to dinner at the home of a legalistic Pharisee, He sat down with his disciples...*without* performing the ceremonial washings prescribed by the Jewish law. His hypocritical host acted shocked and offended. Jesus knew what his host was thinking and called him on it.

Jesus said that the leaders were only concerned about cleaning what others see. They wash cups and plates sparkling clean, but inside they are filled with maggoty greed and sin. (Luke 11: 39-41)

Then Jesus proceeded to tell these religious nobles that they needed to turn both their pockets and their hearts inside out and give generously to the poor. Jesus wanted not just their dishes to be clean but their lives to reflect love for others.

Jesus called it like He saw it. He told them that they kept meticulous books, tithing on every nickel and dime, but managed to find loopholes for getting around basic matters of justice and God's love (Luke 11:41).

Jesus told them that loving others was more important than their meticulous bookkeeping. He finished in verse 52 adding:

"You're hopeless, you religion scholars!
You took the key of knowledge,
but instead of unlocking doors, you locked them.
You won't go in yourself and won't let anyone else in either."

Yikes...Can you imagine being with Jesus that day? I cringe each time I read these words. Nearly choking on their grapes, I envision John and James–the Sons of Thunder, who were known for being loud–cheering quietly on the inside. Even still I bet their eyes were fixed on their food to avoid the stinging stare of the powerful Pharisees.

And big, burly Peter–the protector for the group–was probably eyeing the nearest exit, formulating an emergency escape route for the twelve. You have to admit, Jesus repeatedly nailed down His point, so there could be no twisting of the points (Torsade de Pointes).

Multiple times we hear in the New Testament that Jesus "spoke with authority." I would say this was one of those times. Jesus loved common men. He loved authenticity. Those who thought they were better than others made Him angry. He came to save everyone.

Some didn't feel they needed to be saved. They felt worthy and acted haughty. This brings me to the question: If Jesus were here with us today, what would He say to our religious leaders?

When common people outside the church look inside the church, what do they see? Do they see people who love God and their neighbors? Do they see us humbly teaching salvation by simple faith?

Or do they see legalistic people–like the Pharisees–who act superior and make salvation complex? While I hope they see love and are extended grace, I've heard they see hypocrisy. Jesus certainly didn't candy coat His words when He saw hypocrisy.

If Christ was invited by our pastor to come to a potluck dinner in our church gym, what would He say to us? Hmm…So I'm just going to be totally honest with you. I'm commonly the person who leads our hospitality team; I also always seem to be in charge of decorations. While Jesus is all about hospitality, I don't think He would care a bit about the décor, which is making me refocus on how I should spend my time.

And maybe that's just the point. I need to humbly ask God how He would have me reach others in love daily. Sometimes I make a simple outreach dinner more complicated than it really needs to be.

Sometimes it takes something startling to wake us up. I think Jesus was trying to rouse the religious leaders with His startling words when He was invited to dinner.

Likewise, the day the grandfather fell from his chair in the labor and delivery waiting room was startling. My husband returned his heart to normal by applying simple principles, running an efficient code blue. This saved the man's life.

It's been years since I have given thought to the simple equation that describes how our heart pumps.

$$\text{Blood Flow (Q)} \times \text{Blood Resistance (R)} = \text{Blood Pressure (P)}$$
$$Q \times R = \Delta P$$

It reminds me of another simple equation that tells us that we are saved by grace, not by works so we shouldn't be proud. Salvation is a gift from God (Ephesians 2:8). This verse summarized in an equation might look like:

$$\text{Faith (F)} + \text{Grace (G)} = \text{Salvation (S)}$$

$$F + G = S$$

Notice that works has no place in the equation. Good works don't add to salvation; bad works don't subtract from salvation. Our works can't save us. Jesus did all the work on the cross.

## THE JOURNEY FORWARD:

Torsade is as deadly to our hearts as legalism is to Christ's church. The day we brought our newborn daughter home, God placed my husband exactly where he was needed to restore a man's life. Where has God placed you today? On our journey forward, might you share the simple, untwisted, message of salvation?

$$Faith + Grace = Salvation$$

# INVISIBLE LIGHT

## CONES AND RODS

*M*ining is a hard job. Mining is also a dark job. On our faith expedition to discover diamonds, some days are both hard and dark. Interestingly, even in the darkest of conditions, there are still tiny bits of light present. Did you know that not all light is visible? It's true!

The light we can see (called visible light) is only a part of the electromagnetic spectrum. There are other types of light (like infrared and ultraviolet) that can't be seen by the naked eye.

Miners can now use night vision goggles with image enhancement technology. These goggles collect all the available light and amplify it so that they can easily see what's happening even in the dark.

If you've ever seen a night vision image, you've probably noticed that it has an eery green glow. This is intentional. When available light is captured and amplified, it's turned into electronic information to be transmitted to the eyes.

Night vision goggles are made with screens that produce green pictures because our eyes are more sensitive to green light. And it's easier to look at green pictures than to look at black-and-white pictures for long periods of time.[1]

Our eyes are intricate works of art containing about 120,000,000 rod cells. These cells are responsible for vision at low light levels. Our eyes also contain about 6,000,000 cone cells. These are responsible for our color vision.

When studying for exams in pharmacy school **c**ones, starting with the letter "**c**," made it easy to remember that **c**ones allowed me to see in **c**olor, which also started with the letter "**c**." Life would be much duller without color. It's amazing to think that God created us so that we can enjoy over 7,000,000 different color shades.[2]

HAVE YOU EVER HAD DAYS WHEN EVERYTHING SEEMED DARK AND colorless? Heavy, shadowy days when you needed something or someone to lighten your mood...to help you see the good in your life, like night vision goggles help you see light in darkness? I sure have.

As we round the bend starting the second half of our faith expedition together, we are looking to Christ. He is the Light of the world. And He wants us to follow Him, so we won't stub our toes and whack our chins as we maneuver through dark days. He tells us that in Him we have light that leads to life (John 8:12).

He's good, and looking to Him and His Word moment by moment amplifies the good, like night vision goggles amplify the light. I have found that with Him we can better see our blessings...like invisible light that becomes visible with the right goggles.

That's why I include scripture in every chapter of this book. It allows us to see blessings we might normally miss...blessings that brighten our days and lighten our loads, giving us a fresh perspective.

Can I be transparent with you? Sometimes when I wake up weighed down, in addition to my Bible and prayer, I need a Godly friend. Someone I can meet for a brisk walk and talk! Likewise, when we're able to help others focus on their blessings, we're living out Matthew 5:14-16, where we're told to be a light to the world like a city on a hilltop that cannot be hidden. Similarly, we are to let our **good deeds shine** out for all to see, so that everyone will praise our heavenly Father.

Our good deeds bring light to others. Of all my senses, I rely most on my sight. If you're like me, we're not alone. In Acts 9:3-18 we read about a man named Saul who was knocked off his high horse by a blinding light and lost his sight for three days. Though God could have taken any one of his five senses, I ask myself why God took his sight.

Perhaps it was so Saul would gain spiritual insight to see who was most important. Where he was once blind to Jesus, he was now able to see Him for who He was, his Lord and Savior. He went from persecutor to proselyte in one blinding moment.

What I love most about the story of Saul is the ending. Jesus called a man named Ananias in a **vision** to go to Saul and lay hands on him so his vision would be restored.

Ananias was hesitant because he had heard about the horrible things Saul had done to Christians in Jerusalem. Even worse, he knew that Saul's visit to Damascus was authorized by leading priests to arrest more Christians.

It must have been hard for Ananias to hear that Saul was chosen by God to take the Good News to the Gentiles, to kings and the people of Israel. Not only did Saul need healed, he needed an encourager. Someone who could reach out and touch him, laying hands on him. Listen to how Ananias responds to God's call and greets Saul in verse 17-18:

"**Brother** Saul, the Lord Jesus, who appeared to you on the road,
has sent me so that you might regain your sight
and be filled with the Holy Spirit."
Instantly something like scales fell from Saul's eyes,
and he regained his sight. Then he got up and was baptized.

This leads me to ask, how can God use us today to help others see spiritually? The answer takes me full circle back to the simplicity of Matthew 5:16 where we're told to "let our **good deeds shine** out for all to **see.**"

## THE JOURNEY FORWARD:

On our journey forward, what good deeds might we be called to complete today? Though it's unlikely that we'll be asked to heal blindness in the same way as Ananias, might we be called to reach out to a stranger or even an enemy with a caring touch? Like night vision goggles, will we help them see light amidst darkness?

## TYLENOL AND TRUTH

On our faith journey we've learned that diamonds are nontoxic. I admit that seems strange when other things like Tylenol® that we swallow regularly can be toxic.

At high doses, Tylenol is highly toxic. How can something so common be so dangerous? That's the question a young lady and her parents asked my husband after she swallowed more than fifty capsules. She had been caught in a bad lie at school, had a bad headache, bad cramps and a bad fight with her boyfriend.

Madison didn't think that Tylenol was "any big deal." And she didn't realize it would hurt her; after all, she had taken it since she was a kid. Even Madison's parents were lulled into a sense of benign familiarity with Tylenol. They weren't alarmed when she told them she had "taken too much."

Her plans for a prom dress, along with her spot on the state track team, dissolved as quickly as the dozens of caplets dissolved in her stomach. Madison was confined to a hospital bed with dialysis waiting for the results from my husband. Dave was waiting for the report from the lab.

Each day Madison's enzymes become more elevated, indicating more liver damage. Her protime, which reflects her body's ability to make clotting factors, continues to rise, putting her at risk for massive bleeds.

My husband shares her family's grief each morning when he sits on the edge of her bed and explains the tragic test results. In less than five percent of patients experiencing this level of Tylenol toxicity, their liver heals. Our family prays for her each night at the dinner table.

THERE IS A SPIRITUAL LESSON BURIED IN THIS TRAGIC STORY. JUST as the little white tablets of Tylenol are common and seem harmless, the little white lies we tell are common and seem harmless. But are they really?

Does God differentiate *little lies* from **big lies**? Though you and I differentiate levels or degrees of lies, scripture does not. Darkness cannot exist in the presence of Light. Lies cannot exist in the presence of Truth.

The issue at hand is much larger. Jesus Himself explains that *if* we are faithful in little things, we will also be faithful in big ones. But if we are dishonest in little things, we won't be honest with greater responsibilities (Luke 16:10).

This prompts me to ask myself if I'm faithful in matters that may seem unimportant and truthful in matters that may seem insignificant. To God the small things matter.

Jesus wants us to succeed in small trials so that we can flourish in larger ones. He's cheering for us to prove ourselves faithful and trustworthy so that He can entrust us with greater spiritual gifts (Luke 19:17). He's thrilled to bless us!

Paul knew that lies were deceptive. Yet like Tylenol little white lies can make us feel better. They can temporarily take away the anxiety or embarrassment. Even still, lies can be fatal to friendships, toxic to marriages and poisonous to children.

That being said, there's a difference between lies and brutal, uncontrolled honesty when considering the feelings of others. While we're not called to lie, we are called to "do unto others as we would want done to us" (Matthew 7:12). This requires wisdom in choosing our words. It also requires verbal restraint. Words, like Tylenol, can be used to heal or to harm.

THE JOURNEY FORWARD:

On your journey forward, the next time you take Tylenol, might you remember that honesty is the best policy? Both our lives and our livers are at stake. Speaking of livers, I'm just dying to give you an update on Madison.

After nearly a month in the hospital, Madison gets to leave just in time for her prom. She received her miracle! Her liver enzymes finally started to return to normal. My husband is hopeful she will make a complete recovery and will even be able to continue to compete in the 400-meter dash. While the records she sets in track may not stand the test of time, truth always will (Proverbs 12:19)?

Note: While truth is unchanging, to respect privacy, names in this chapter were changed.

# PARESTHESIA

## A PRICKLY PECULIAR PERCEPTION

*a*s you sit reading has your foot ever fallen asleep? What a strange sensation when your fingers feel your leg, but your leg doesn't feel your fingers. What once was a dual sensation is now a unilateral experience of your fingers. It's such a prickly, peculiar perception; laughing comes naturally, as you struggle to your *feet* in a *feat* to walk.

Your foot is still connected to the end of your leg; you've just forgotten how to use it. As you try to stomp some life back into it, you're given a bit of insight regarding patients with paralysis.

You're telling your leg and foot to walk, but the message seems disconnected and garbled. A humorously simple task is complicated by the sensation that your foot is three times its normal size and seems to weigh more than a bowling ball. Why? You have unknowingly applied direct pressure compressing a nerve, causing what doctors call "paresthesia."

JUST AS OUR EXTREMITIES MAY FEEL NUMB DUE TO COMPRESSION of a nerve, we may feel numb due to lack of connection to the Holy Spirit. Emotional numbness temporarily immobilizes us, much like a foot that has fallen asleep. When we're numb sometimes simple tasks seem difficult, just like the simple task of walking seems difficult if we have no feeling in our leg.

Though we may look the same outwardly, as our foot does when it is "sleeping," we can feel strangely alienated. Just as our foot seems much larger than it is in reality, our problems can seem much larger. It can seem like everyone is jabbing at us. Likewise, when our foot is asleep, we can feel a jabbing sensation. Our perception can be distorted. We can be...

numb to our blessings...

numb to our family...

numb to our spouse...

numb to our friends...

numb to our coworkers.

Just as we can stomp our foot when it has fallen asleep, we can stomp through our day devoid of delight. If you were to experience prolonged numbness in a limb, you would consult your doctor. Likewise, if you experience prolonged depression, consult your doctor.

As a pharmacist I can tell you that depression, due to chemical imbalances in the brain, is very treatable. There are numerous types of antidepressants; if one doesn't relieve the pain of depression, other classes of antidepressants can be prescribed.

For the type of unhappiness that is transient (much like your leg falling asleep) here are a few remedies that I've found useful in my own life. Rather than focusing on my own frustrations and hurts, I look around me for others who are hurting...others who might need a listening ear, help watching a kiddo, a smile, a compliment, a hug, or a home-cooked meal.

I remember my Mom always saying, "You can't out-give God." We find this truth in *Luke 6:38. Eugene Peterson, who paraphrased *The Message Bible*, says it this way:

"Give away your life; you'll find life given back,
but not merely given back—
given back with bonus and blessing.
Giving, not getting, is the way.
Generosity begets generosity."

I like bonuses and I'm always open to blessings. How about you? I am amazed at the ways I receive these "bonuses and blessings." When I find the time to make a meal to take to someone who is hurting, I'm energized so that I'm able to accomplish everything I need to fit into my day caring for my own family.

God gives me a clarity to move forward, where I might otherwise be drawn off task and struggle. What God returns to me may not be tangible or something that I can see, but it's no less real than the things I can't see but know exist beyond the horizon. When I am driving down the highway at 70 MPH I know that the road exists, even if I can't see it beyond my headlights.

We can also learn from the example of the churches in Macedonia found in 2 Corinthians 8:2:

"Though they have been going
through much trouble and hard times,
they have mixed their wonderful joy
with their deep poverty,
and the result has been an overflow of giving to others."

This amazes me. Even though they were experiencing "deep poverty," they were generously rich toward others. And they were blessed for it!

Is there an area in your life where you're poor or lacking? As a working mother of two toddlers, I lack spare time yet somehow, God has multiplied what little I have, making it more than enough. He takes my two-goldfish-and-five-crouton time and talents and multiplies them just like He did when He fed 5,000 men, not including their wives and children (Mark 6:30-44). To Him be the glory!

THE JOURNEY FORWARD:

On our journey forward, the next time your foot falls asleep might you be moved to walk in love? While numbness lasts only minutes, love is eternal (1 Corinthians 13:8, 13). Is there a friend in need with whom you could reconnect, bringing a sparkle to their day…like a diamond?

# MY FAVORITE COMFORT FOOD

*M*ining for **Diamonds In Our Days** works up an appetite for the good. I crave good things…and that includes good food. Potatoes find their way into many of my meals. Did you know that potatoes are one of the healthiest foods around? They're an excellent source of essential vitamins, like B6, that help build your brain and protect your heart.

Because potatoes offer nearly forty grams of carbohydrates per serving, they're among the best energy sources available. And they're rich in fiber, containing nearly fifteen percent of our daily fiber need.

What few people realize is one medium potato contains nearly ten percent of the protein we require each day. Pound per pound potatoes are also one of most economical foods available. They're the number one vegetable crop in the world. Available year-round, they're harvested somewhere every month of the year.

For me, potatoes are one of my favorite comfort foods. It's likely that others feel this way too as the potato's scientific name is *Solanum tuberosum. Solanum* is derived from a Latin word for soothing.[1]

The potato is a healthy vegetable until we smother it with yummy butter or make it into French fries...or my personal favorite–potato chips. How can something that starts off so good become so bad?

SOMETIMES MY MOTIVES HAVE A LOT IN COMMON WITH POTATOES. They start out being a great source of energy. Like a potato, they provide fuel for good works. But my healthy motivation to serve God can become laden with self-serving oil, much like chips or fries.

What started out as a good work with pure motives becomes a work done for praise. We are told to be careful. Good deeds done publicly, to be admired, will result in the loss of our heavenly reward from our Father (Matthew 6:1).

Being rewarded here on earth feels as good as potato chips taste. It feels great to be acknowledged. Working silently behind the scenes isn't nearly as fun as taking in the limelight.

It's tough to offer your time to help others when what you really want is time to relax. "Laboring for the Lord"–with no thanks here on earth–might be as enjoyable as eating a baked potato with no toppings.

Like barbecue potato chips taste good, complaining feels good. It's tempting to complain. Likewise, it's tempting to choose fries over a wholesome potato. But just as there are rewards for eating heart-healthy foods, there are rewards for works that go unnoticed here on earth. We're told not to call attention to our acts of charity but to give gifts in private; then our Heavenly Father will reward us (Matthew 6:4).

So we're much wiser to store our treasures in heaven, where it won't rust or be stolen. Most importantly we're reminded that wherever our treasure is, the desires of our heart will also be (Matthew 6:21).

I think God knows that a **headful** of recognition always leaves us wanting for more, much like a **handful** of potato chips. And if we look to others to fulfill the desires of our heart, we'll always be hungry for more. We can't make our meals from just chips, nor can we feel eternally full apart from God.

THE JOURNEY FORWARD:

We all have moments when we indulge. I admit, saturated food tastes as good as being saturated with praise. It's difficult to exercise self-control and refrain from loading up on chips...or to refrain from unloading the chips on our shoulders when our hard work goes unnoticed. Be encouraged. Though we are not saved by our good works, we will be rewarded the good we do for others (Matthew 16:27).

# NOSE AND HAIR

*D*id you know both the nose on your face and the hair on your head lengthen with time? It's a medical fact that the cartilage of your nose lengthens each decade. It is a medical myth, however, that the more often you have your hair trimmed, the faster it will grow. Because hair itself is dead, it never *grows*. The hair follicle, however, does produce more hair and thus, hair *lengthens*.

We perceive that our hair is growing. Some people insist their hair grows fast; others are convinced that their hair grows slow. The reality is that everyone's hair *lengthens* an average of about two to four inches per year. Hair rarely ever exceeds thirty-six inches in length.

We shed about 100 hairs each day. Every seven years, the hair follicle that produces hair dies. Even if we never trimmed our hair, it would reach its maximum length by the seventh year, then the follicle would be replaced.[1] Even on bad hair days, when each strand has a mind of its own, the strands on our heads can point us toward God.

JESUS LOVINGLY SHARES THAT GOD CARES FOR US SO MUCH HE knows exactly how many hairs we have on our head (Luke 12:7). As a child, I remember being fascinated by this fact. I looked at the hair that was stuck in my brush each morning thinking that Jesus was really good at subtraction. As the day progressed occasionally I would yank one out just to make sure He was paying attention. Being a middle child, I didn't want His focus to drift from me.

As adults we might ask ourselves why Jesus chooses to talk about the dead hairs on our heads. I think it's because He wants us to completely comprehend how much He cherishes us, because He explains in verse 6:

> "What is the price of five sparrows
> —two copper coins?"
> "Yet God does not forget a single one of them...
> So don't be afraid; you are more valuable to God
> than a whole flock of sparrows."

Jesus came down from heaven to make sure we know how much our heavenly Father loves us. This perfect love casts out all fear (1 John 4:18). We can rest reassured, knowing He treasures us from the hair on our head to the hairs on our toes.

May I share a secret with you?

This passage also makes me smile inside. Since childhood I've been self-conscious about my hair. Perhaps it's because my sister, Kathy, has luxuriously thick brunette tresses…the kind you see on shampoo commercials. My hair is thin and fine without much body.

Even worse, the color was what my mom called "dishwater blonde." As a child I would have much preferred true blonde hair like Shelly Morgan, who lived just across the alley.

When I fully grasp that God has numbered every dishwater blonde strand, I light up knowing that I am cherished by my Creator. That's a fact that's worth more than…well, a lifetime of good hair days.

## THE JOURNEY FORWARD:

On our journey forward, know that God loves you and has every hair on your head numbered. The next time you comb your hair, might you be reminded of your value in God's sight? You are worth more than every diamond on this planet.

Is there some way you can share that love today? Perhaps when you visit the hair salon next, you can be generous in your tip and share with your hairdresser how God loves them.

# REVIA®

*R*eVia®. It's the Latin word meaning "new life." It's also the name that has been appropriately given to a drug that's used to free patients from the disease of alcoholism.

It is an "opioid blocker," which means that it blocks the opioid receptors in a patient's brain. When they drink alcohol it's unable to bind to the receptor as it would normally.

The result? Alcoholics on ReVia® don't find drinking to be euphoric. They don't feel good when they drink. Alcohol no longer has the pizzazz that it once had.

Not all of us have experienced the craving to drink as alcoholics do, but we have all experienced the common cold. When you can't smell because you're congested, eating your favorite meal doesn't have the same satisfaction. You crave less because it is less appealing.

The same holds true for the alcoholic on ReVia. Compared to patients taking a placebo, ReVia® patients have twice the success in giving up the bottle and have half the number of relapses.

If there are relapse periods, they drink for half the number of days and drink half the number of drinks per day.[1] Bottom line, we've discovered the receptor in the brain responsible for much of the euphoria attributed to alcohol.

THE PHARMACEUTICAL INDUSTRY HAS ISOLATED AND DESIGNED many drugs that block specific receptors. Wouldn't it be great if the clergy could isolate and design meds that would block the pleasure of specific sins? And wouldn't life be easier if we didn't have to battle the desire to sin?

Sometimes we may think that we face the battle of sin alone, but we don't. Paul was one of the holiest men to ever grace the pages of the Bible, yet even he wrestled with his flesh, sharing in Romans 7:19:

> "I want to do what is good, but I don't.
> I don't want to do what is wrong, but I do it anyway."

He's transparent, explaining his ups and downs, sharing that he has this internal pull toward sin. Despite his love for God's law, for the next several verses he details his struggle, saying that there's a power within him that is at war with his mind. That power makes him miserable and a slave to sin (Romans 7:20-25).

Paul came to the conclusion that every day he woke up, he would experience this internal tug of war between his flesh and the spirit of God that lived in him. He encourages us, sharing that the temptations we face are experienced by us all. Then he reassures us, saying in 1 Corinthians 10:13:

"All you need to remember is that God will never let you down;
he'll never let you be pushed past your limit;
he'll always be there to help you come through it."

This verse taken in context reassures us that with regards to overcoming temptation, God will provide an escape route...a detour around sin and bad choices. Conversely, this verse taken out of context can do harm when we wrongly apply it to those who are experiencing overwhelming tragedies and spout: "Well, God never gives you more than you can handle."

So when it comes to temptation the question is, will I choose sin or Him? If I fail today, tomorrow God will offer me a second chance to succeed.


THE JOURNEY FORWARD:

There is no drug like ReVia® that can block our enjoyment of all sin but we do have all three persons of the Godhead on our side. We couldn't ask for a better recovery care team!

On our journey forward, though we can't swallow Psalm 51:10 in capsule form like ReVia®, it's one sentence that's easy to remember and pray when we face temptation.

"Create in me a clean heart, O God.
Renew a loyal spirit within me."

# VITAMINS AND JEWELRY

Choices. Choices. Choices. There are so many fun options my preschooler has in a day…one of which is the vitamin shape and color she chooses.

We have animal-shaped vitamins and Flintstone vitamins. Seems simple enough…but no! There are lions and bears, doggies and kitties, giraffes and elephants. And a single bottle of Flintstone vitamins offers several choices as well. There is Fred, Barney, Pebbles and Bamm-Bamm. As mothers themselves, Wilma and Betty had enough good sense to stay out of the picture…or in this case, the bottle.

"Vitamins are good for my tummy," my daughter insists. Then she hops around the kitchen imitating the bunny vitamin that she holds in her hand before nibbling off the large ears. Alyssa prefers vitamins over vegetables any day.

Likewise, many folks think that vitamins insure they have a healthy diet. This simply isn't true. A vitamin provides the **R**ecommended **D**aily **A**llowances (RDA) of vitamins and some minerals, but they are not the building blocks for a stable diet. In essence they're the mortar that holds the building stones together. But you can't build a structure out of mortar alone; you need bricks.

Since I'm no mason, and we are on an expedition to discover **Diamonds In Our Days**, I like to think of vitamins as diamond jewelry. The outfits we choose vary. Some need accessories; others don't. Likewise, some diets need to be supplemented while others don't. But clothing is always more essential than jewelry.

I've never forgotten to put on my pants, though I've forgotten to put on a necklace. Similarly, I've never forgotten to wear a shirt, but I've found myself halfway through my day when I realize I've forgotten earrings.

Carbohydrates, proteins and fats are the essentials. They are like the pants, shirts and shoes of our diet. We can't do without them and no number of accessories will cover the fact that they're missing!

JUST AS WE HAVE BASIC NUTRITIONAL NEEDS FOR PHYSICAL health, we have basic "nutritional" needs for spiritual health. Scripture is the cornerstone for a healthy spirit.

God's Word is an essential component of our soul's diet just as shirts are an essential component of our wardrobe. Though there are many fantastic Christian authors, none surpass God Himself. Jesus tells us that it takes more than bread to stay alive. It takes a steady diet of God's word (Matthew 4:4). Sermons spoken by our pastors that contain scripture and mentors who remind us of scripture are important ways we are fed.

As for the issue of spiritual diets, John 6:27 advises us not to waste our energy striving for "perishable" food. Instead he tells us to work for the food that sticks with us, nourishing us forever. The Son of Man's nourishment is guaranteed to last forever, which is more than any label on a bottle of vitamins can claim.

When we're hungry, we don't head for the medicine cabinet for a plate of vitamins, we head to the refrigerator for a plate of food. Likewise, when our spirits are starved and we have an emptiness that nothing seems to fill, Jesus tells us that He is the bread of life and those who come to Him won't ever go hungry (John 6:35).

Facebook won't fulfill us. T.V. won't captivate us forever. And shopping won't satisfy our spirits. Only the Living Word can support spiritual life, just as nutritional building blocks of carbohydrates, proteins and fats support physical life.

Other Christian books (like this one) could be equated to vitamins. They can't sustain life nor can they can't fully satiate our soul's appetite. They may supplement our diet of the Word, like vitamins, but they won't ever replace it.

THE JOURNEY FORWARD:

As a pharmacist, I recommend a daily multivitamin along with a healthy diet. On our journey forward, when we pray "The Lord's Prayer" and ask that God "give us this day our daily bread," might you think about our more important daily spiritual bread?

# BELLY BUTTONS

## THE ANATOMY OF ABIDING

*O*ur journey is a faith expedition but it's also a fun expedition. So tonight I had to laugh when my daughter was playing in the bathtub and wondered out loud: "Mommy, what belly button for?"

I'm asked a lot of questions every day as a pharmacist, but this was a new one for me. In an attempt to stall a few seconds to think of an answer, I gently corrected her grammar. "What *are* belly buttons for? (Long pause on my part.) Well…that's where your umbilical cord was attached when you were in Mommy's tummy. Before you were born, Mommy fed you through that cord like you drink milk through a straw."

Alyssa cocked her head and scrunched up her sweet little nose, obviously dumbfounded. "What?" She asked. I wondered how to simplify my answer. "That's where Mommy fed you when you were in my tummy."

I thought she would be more confused, but to my surprise she seemed appeased. I bent down to hand a foam alphabet sponge to my son, who sat behind her in the tub. He immediately started sucking it and flashed his toothless grin. When I looked back toward my daughter, she had a spoon from her tea set and was feeding her belly button.

ANATOMY, PHYSIOLOGY AND THE FETUS. THREE DIFFICULT concepts for a three-year-old. While we understand that the function of an umbilical cord is to nourish an unborn child, there are concepts of spiritual nourishment that I still find difficult as an adult.

This morning I was reminded of one of Jesus' many beautiful stories when reading my Bible. It was about a vineyard and is found in John 15. There Jesus tells us that those who *abide* in Him will be so nourished that they will bear *much fruit*. It sounds so beautifully simple.

A vine is attached to a branch and nourished much like my daughter was attached to me and nourished in my womb. Both of these attachments seem effortless and both result in beautiful growth.

Likewise, when we abide in Christ we are nourished, producing spiritual fruit. When I *abide*, I'm at peace. I feel as close and connected to my Creator as a child must feel in the womb. I am warm, secure and safe.

Another word for abide is *to rest*. Do you find that it's hard *to rest* in a harsh world that promotes business and perpetual busyness? I do. Jesus did too.

He understands that there are meals to be made, kids to be bathed and bills to be paid. And between loads of laundry to be done and lullabies to be sung, He understands that we need to rest in Him. So how do we *abide*, staying connected to Him like a vine to a branch and an unborn baby to their mother?

I am learning more every day about abiding and it's super exciting. This year I have chosen "abide" as *My One Word*. My choice is based on a book entitled *My One Word*, written by Mike Ashcroft and Rachel Olsen. They challenge readers to choose one word that represents what they most need God to change in them—and focus on it for an entire year.[1]

I love the Biblical encouragement and real-life stories from people who've been transformed by this spiritual exercise. I'm learning to abide in life's smudged, imperfect moments. And I can tell you that I'm seeing Godly diamond moments more than ever before by consciously *resting* in Him.

I'm amazed at the insights He allows me to see when I slow down and He shows up. Sometimes He shows up in a majestic sunset that I take (and make) the time to watch. Other times He shows up in a silly question from my daughter that I take the time to ponder.

Which brings me back to the original bath-time question: "What are belly buttons for?" Well...maybe they're to remind us that just as we were once connected to our earthly mother for nourishment, we now need to stay connected to our heavenly Father for nourishment.

THE JOURNEY FORWARD:

Can you disconnect from your cell phone and connect to God right now in prayer? Perhaps you can find time to rest someplace different than you would normally relax. Maybe you can take a blanket outside on your porch. If it's cold, warm a blanket in the dryer first, then wrap yourself in it.

If it's morning, can you watch the sun rise or listen to the birds chirp? God hides diamonds everywhere in His creation (Romans 1:20).

Rest.

Relax.

Recline.

Go on.

Work will wait.

# M & M'S

*Y*ummy munchies are always good to bring on trips. I appreciate you joining me on this faith journey. If you were by my side, I would share some of my favorite snack candies with you. M & M's are so fun.

Did you know how M & M's got their name? Back in 1941 Forrest **M**ars (of the Mars candy company) struck a deal with Bruce **M**urrie (son of famed Hershey president, William Murrie). They developed a hard-shelled candy with chocolate at the center, naming this new candy **M & M's**.

Coincidentally, my favorite medical conference is the weekly **M & M** conference. While the candy and the conference may share the same name, they're very different. **M & M** conference is an opportunity each week for different medical specialties to present difficult patient cases and discuss medical options, considering both the **M**orbidity and **M**ortality of their patients.

The goal is to find the best possible treatment for a patient, with dozens of specialized doctors weighing in. I love to see the medical team come together for the good of the patient. It's a powerful ministry that has saved thousands of lives. Oftentimes it's the highlight of my week.

It's easy to define mortality at any age, but morbidity is a bit harder, as it focuses on quality of life which changes with each decade. The expectations of an eighty-year-old are very different from the expectations of an eighteen-year-old.

Every year the CDC studies M & M.[1] This year it took nearly 500 pages to report on what I can summarize in five words. It's good news...wanna hear it?

We are healthier living longer.

WHILE EARTHLY PHYSICIANS FOCUS ON IMPROVING MORTALITY AND morbidity, the Great Physician focuses on salvation and sanctification. As Christians we are familiar with salvation. When we openly profess that Jesus is Lord, believing in our hearts that God raised Him from the dead, we will be saved (Romans 10:9).

And we learn in Titus 3:5 that He saved us not because we deserve it but because He is merciful. He washed away our sins and gave us a new life through the Holy Spirit.

Salvation brings us immortality and we're born into God's family. Our names are written on our birth certificates, just as our names are written in the Book of Life (Revelation 20:15).

So while salvation is easy to define, sanctification can be a bit more difficult. There are many descriptions of sanctification; all involve spiritual maturity or becoming more Christ-like. In order to grow in maturity we are told to crave pure spiritual milk like newborn babies. Then we will grow into "a full experience of salvation" (1 Peter 2:2)

I like the way Peter speaks of "the full experience of salvation" because this is what sanctification is all about! Fully living is thriving abundantly and living our best lives.

When I was in high school, I attended an interdenominational youth group called *New Creations*. Its name was based on 2 Corinthians 5:17 where Paul speaks about sanctification, telling us that those who know Christ are made new. The old things are erased.

As we grow older, try as we might, some of the results of aging can't be physically erased. But spiritually we can be made new. Paul talks about leaving a sinful past behind. He encourages sanctification, explaining that we have been given a fresh start.

Since God lives in us, we're called to live by a higher standard. Just because we can skate by with something doesn't necessarily mean it's good for us. Paul shares that if he went around doing whatever he thought he could get by with, he'd be a slave to his whims (1 Corinthians 6:12-13).

Much like my heavenly Father, my earthly father always encouraged each of his three children to make good decisions and to "put one foot in front of the other." This basic approach is how I see sanctification. It's the process of putting one foot in front of the other. And–with the help of the Holy Spirit–walking toward Christ, daily reading His Word, praying and learning how to love others by His example.

## THE JOURNEY FORWARD:

On our journey forward in sanctification, each decade brings increasing morbidity, as our physical body fails. But quite the opposite is true in our spiritual journey. With each step we take towards God, becoming more like His Son and maturing in our faith, the quality of our life increases! Even the mortality of our bodies marks a new, better beginning in heaven.

# FIBROMYALGIA

*F*ibromyalgia. A dozen letters that describe a dozen generalized symptoms, which leave nearly 10,000,000 people in pain.

If you've ever had a pounding headache, making you more sensitive to loud noises and bright lights, you can better understand the "heightened amplification of pain" fibromyalgia patients bravely bear. Due to abnormalities in how pain signals are processed by their brain, those with fibromyalgia experience pain more intensely.

Chronic aching muscles are common for people with FM, but because their muscles look perfectly healthy, it's very hard to diagnose.

We don't know the cause, though it's thought that half the risk is inherited and half is due to the environment. Recently we've learned that gluten may play a role.

The treatment is vague and difficult. Many doctors disagree on the best management because their patients have such acute complaints. Common recommendations are to eat healthy, sleep plenty and exercise regularly.[1] This is difficult for patients to hear when they have gone to their doctor with complaints of hurting all over (which prevents exercising) and not sleeping well. I have a heart for those who suffer with fibromyalgia.

WHILE WE MAY NOT *PHYSICALLY* SUFFER WITH HEIGHTENED sensitivity to physical pain, we may have areas where we're more *emotionally* sensitive due to past experiences. A dear friend of mine was hurt growing up with an ultra-critical father. I have empathy for Jennifer, as my dad always believed I could do anything.

Knowing of her past hurts, I better understand that she has a heightened *emotional* sensitivity to criticism–especially from males. I've seen how this has negatively impacted the decisions she's made.

Because she's in pain, Jen has responded in ways that have fractured her family and her marriages. She carries an invisible pain much like patients who have fibromyalgia.

My dear friend is not alone. Many of us have been hurt; sometimes it was purposeful and other times it was done without malicious intent. The truth is, hurting people hurt others. And hurting people are often also more sensitive to pain.

Do you have an area of your life that still hurts? I do. The pain that I have experienced does make me more emotionally sensitive. I recognize this and have empathy for those who hurt both physically and emotionally.

Physicians may struggle to fully comprehend invisible pain, but know that the Great Physician understands. He loves you and wants to help. I have always found Him ready to listen when I have tears that only He sees.

God listens when we are too embarrassed and too tired to know how we are going to make it through the next week, and thinking about the next year is unfathomable (1 John 5:14). Have you been hurt in a specific area? If so, know that it's normal to be hypersensitive to that same type of pain.

Find a counselor. Grant yourself grace to heal. The Great Physician always dispenses grace. The apostle Luke was also a physician. Only in his gospel do we learn of a woman who hemorrhaged for twelve years.

Dr. Luke doesn't hold back when he shares that this dear woman had spent every penny she had on fellow doctors, who bled her finances while doing nothing for her bleeding (Luke 8:43-47).

Undoubtedly she was anemic from blood loss. With low hemoglobin her cells lacked oxygen, making her chronically lethargic. She was probably *weak* every day of the *week*. Yet somehow she found the strength to push through a crowd to touch the fringe on Jesus' robe. And He stopped.

She sought Jesus, then Jesus sought her!

Never mind that Christ was on His way to the house of a V.I.P. named Jairus. Never mind that His apostles were aggravated by Him stopping to ask who had touched Him.

When no one stepped forward, exasperated Peter spoke up explaining that they were trying to manage crowds of people and that dozens had touched Him. But Jesus persisted, knowing that someone had touched Him differently as He felt power leaving Him.

Then this frail woman stepped forward and knelt before Jesus, trembling. In front of everyone she blurted out her story—why she touched Him and how at that same moment, she was healed. Then Jesus said in *verse 48:

> "'Daughter, you took a risk trusting me,
> and now you're healed and whole.
> **Live well, live blessed!'**"

I love those four words: "Live well, live blessed!" But how do we live well and live blessed if we–unlike the woman–are not instantly healed?

The most difficult question is, "Why aren't we healed when others are?" It doesn't seem fair. While I don't have the answers, I find it assuring that Paul didn't either.

In fact later Paul shares that he too had a chronic condition. Three times he prayed, begging for healing. All three times he was told "no." Perhaps more hurtful was the reason he was given. It was to keep him humble. That must have been hard to hear.

Instead of curing him, God reminded him in 2 Corinthians 12:9 that His grace is all that he needed. After this Paul tells us that he embraced his weaknesses so that Christ's power could work through him. He shares verse 10:

> "That's why I take pleasure in my weaknesses,
>     and in the insults, hardships, persecutions,
>         and troubles that I suffer for Christ.
>     For when I am weak, then I am strong."

Honestly, I struggle with this, but Paul certainly inspires me. He also gives me perspective on the poor woman in scripture, who bled for over 624 weeks. Even in her *weeks* of *weak*ness, she found the strength to pursue Jesus.

She was considered "unclean" and, by law, alienated by her fellow Jews due to the bleeding. This must have made her profoundly lonely and depressed.

She was physically, financially and emotionally drained. Her weakness inspires me to find the strength to press close to Him. For the rest of her life, don't you think that this dear woman had a heart for those who were excluded?

She probably was also sensitive to the pain of alienation. If someone gave her an unwelcoming glance, it may have brought back horrible memories. This would be normal, even expected, given the pain she experienced.

Likewise, my dear friend from college has a painful gouge in her heart from her father's harsh criticisms. She longs for a loving husband to fill the void left by her dad. But it's a hole that can only be filled and healed by the Great Physician, who can make her both whole and holy.

I hurt for her and I understand her. Do you find there is some correlation with your hurt and your need for healing? Just like patients with fibromyalgia I'm learning where I'm sensitive, along with my dear friend. This helps her and me better understand both our *actions* and our **re***actions*…and the impact on those we love.


THE JOURNEY FORWARD:

While this journey through pain is arduous, like mining deep within the earth for diamonds, the Great Physician sees invisible pain. Unlike your human physician, who may not have an open appointment for weeks, God is always available.

On our journey forward, do you have an area where you need His healing touch? He offers to be our Jehovah Rapha–which is His Hebrew name for "the God who heals" (Exodus 15:26). Make time to spend with Him today.

# PEARL PYLE

## AND THE FUNNY PAGES

e've traveled a long way in our faith journey to quarry **Diamonds In Our Days**. Sometimes there are diamond mines right in our neighborhood. Growing up, Pearl Pyle lived three doors down Richmond Avenue. I distinctly remember my mom instructing my little brother that he could go as far as Mrs. Pyle's on his bicycle…but no further. Barney always was one to live on the edge; perhaps that's why Pearl was his good buddy. He spent a lot of time at her house.

Pearl was pleasantly plump and Doc was the light of her life. They both had silver-gray hair. Doc's belly was so big it nearly drug on the floor. Oh, did I mention that Doc had no arms? He had four legs and fur.

As a Schnauzer he was mild-mannered except when it came to his Nilla Wafers® and Sara Lee Pound Cake®. His two adopted brothers–both strays that Pearl rescued–knew they were second fiddle.

Mrs. Pyle was generous with both smiles and snacks. She always had a reserve cake in the freezer, and my brother soon learned that all it took was one grin and the party would begin.

Pearl was fun loving...until she started having her little strokes. At first they weren't incapacitating. She would just call everyone "Doc" and everything a "pan handle." Funny what words she remembered.

Then things became worse and she couldn't live alone. We had to say farewell to Pearl as our neighbor when she left the block. I never heard Pearl say good-bye even before her stroke; she always smiled, winked and chuckled, "I'll see you in the funny pages!"

TODAY WHEN I THINK OF PEARL, I AM SADDENED KNOWING HOW strokes steal and silence those we love. Strokes physically cripple our minds just as sin spiritually corrupts our testimony.

Paul was straightforward in distinguishing two types of people in Romans 8:5 explaining:

"For they that are after the flesh do mind the things of the flesh;
but they that are after the Spirit the things of the Spirit.
For to be carnally minded is death;
but to be spiritually minded is life and peace."

This leads me to ask myself the easy question: Which would I rather have–death or life and peace? Really the more difficult question is, how do I become spiritually minded, choosing life and peace?

Paul sheds some light on the subject in 1 Corinthians 2:11-12 explaining that we must know Christ and be filled with the Holy Spirit in order to be spiritually minded. No one can know God's thoughts except God's own Spirit. And God has actually given us His Spirit. With His Spirit living within us we actually have the mind of Christ...a portion of His very thoughts (Romans 8:15-16).

Christ living within us transforms our minds and our thoughts. Paul explains that we are to offer our ordinary, everyday, smudged moments to God as an offering. He tells us that God most wants us to embrace Him.

We are not to be well adjusted to this world and its culture. Rather we are to fix our attention on God. Then He will change us from the inside out. In responding to God's call quickly, we are set apart from the world. The culture around us can drag us down, while God lifts us up...always bringing out the best in us (*Romans 12:2). He helps us to mature into all we could ever hope to be!

THE JOURNEY FORWARD:

When I think of Pearl, I remember how strokes paralyzed her vocabulary and speech, just as sin can paralyze our walk and witness to the world. On our journey forward, what paralyzes you most?

Like Pearl who was generous with Nilla Wafers®, God is generous with healing, telling us in 2 Corinthians 5:17: "This means that anyone who belongs to Christ has become a new person. The old life is gone; a new life has begun!" Here's to saying good-bye to my old self...or as Pearl would say "I'll see you in the funny pages."

# PRUNEY WRINKLES

## AND A PRUNEY PROPHET

*T*oday on our faith journey, God amazed me again by how He created us...specifically in the design of our fingers and toes. And while I often stand in front of my fridge with the door wide open looking for something yummy, I rarely have moments when I'm looking for prunes.

So you may be asking, what do prunes have in common with fingers and toes? Very little...unless you spend over an hour in water, then the two appear to have loads in common. My daughter, who loves to play in the bathtub, marvels at this simple phenomenon.

Have you ever wondered why only our fingers and toes become wrinkled? Why not our earlobes and elbows, our arms or our legs? Like treads on a car tire, the wrinkles on our fingers and toes are God's way of allowing us to have a better grip on objects…things that we might need to hold with our hands (like wet fish) or balance on with our feet (like wet rocks).

Did you know what causes our fingers and toes to develop these "treads"? Our skin *appears* to shrivel because blood vessels under the surface of the skin constrict. The resulting loss of volume in each finger causes the skin to temporarily shrink inward, forming wrinkles. God's designs are intricate and incredible. He thinks of everything and gives us just what we need… when we most need it.

YOU'RE PROBABLY WONDERING HOW WRINKLED TOES COULD OFFER a shriveled ounce of spiritual insight. If you turn to the book of Jonah, you'll find the answer submerged in the four short chapters, documenting the three long days, that the too proud prophet spent in the belly of one big fish.

I've had times when quite simply I wanted to do what seemed good to me. I shushed that still, small voice in my spirit that knew I wasn't aligned with God. I've told discernment to buckle in and takes its place in the back seat while I drove. God is so patient with me.

Have there been times in your life when you insisted on driving, leaving God in the dust on the side of the road waving a caution sign? Even when our disobedience takes us on a detour, we can cry out to God like Jonah did.

We each know what it feels like to be buried "beneath wild,

stormy waves" (Jonah 2:3). Though we may never have had seaweed wrapped around our heads (Jonah 2:5), we each have experienced times we feel tangled and trapped in our life situations. At those times we too can call out to God, asking that He snatches us from the jaws of death (Jonah 2:6).

Like Jonah our salvation comes from the Lord alone (Jonah 2:9). The story of Jonah reminds us that God can deliver us from impossible situations just as He did Jonah when He ordered the fish to spit him onto the beach (Jonah 2:10).

Because the wonder-filled fish story has been familiar to us since childhood, we sometimes forget to envision what being in the stomach of an aquatic mammal for over seventy hours would do to our skin.

Picture even being in the pool for that long. Add to the water hydrochloric acid, potassium chloride and sodium chloride (salt) to form gastric juices. In mammals these stomach secretions have the same pH as battery acid and can dissolve both metal and wood! Having been swallowed by a whale, Jonah was treated to a full-body chemical peel from the Spa of Hard Knocks.

The day the Lord ordered the whale to hurl Jonah onto dry land, Jonah decided to obey God and proclaim the message God gave him (Jonah 3:1). Suppose for a moment when on your way to work you saw this pruney prophet, who was probably still wearing the same vomit-encrusted clothes.

Imagine how he would smell.

Imagine how his waterlogged voice would sound as he shouted to the crowds that God was going to destroy them in forty days (Jonah 3:4). Who would want to be anywhere near this angry, stinking madman?

Miraculously, the people of Nineveh listened, believed Jonah and turned to God. They proclaimed a citywide fast and dressed in burlap to show they were sorry and ready to change. We learn that everyone did this—rich and poor, famous and obscure, leaders and followers (Jonah 3:5-6).

The whole sinful city was sincerely sorry. The citizens of Nineveh regretted their choices and were contrite. Have you ever stopped to imagine why? I venture to say that Jonah's choice in clothing and his general hygiene was not endearing nor was his irritable personality. The prophet didn't even like the Ninevites. He detested them and wanted them destroyed (Jonah 4:1).

I wonder how we would react to a man like Jonah. Here in America, a proud world power, would we repent and turn to God as did Nineveh, an ancient world power? Would our president be seen on all of the major networks, urging Democrats and Republicans alike to fast and pray?

The miracle of the book of Jonah is not the fact that **a man** was swallowed by a fish (which some Biblical scholars question). Then he repented and lived to tell about it. The more eternal miracle is that **all the men** of Nineveh swallowed their pride, repented and lived to tell about it.

Do Nineveh and America share more in common than the same number of letters and the fact that their names rhyme? I believe that they do.

I also believe that God can teach us through the life of Jonah.

As I reflect on what I can learn from his encounter, I've decided I'd rather swallow my pride and follow God's will even though it's unlikely that I'll be swallowed by a whale. Is there an area in your life that you have hesitated to surrender to God? Can you ask Him to lead...and then follow Him?

Honestly, there are issues in my life that I have surrendered to Him one day, but the very next day I take control of them again. I think this is common. It reminds me of an old hymn, *"Where He Leads Me I Will Follow."* [1] It's based on Matthew 8:19 with the resounding chorus:

"Where He leads me I will follow,
Where He leads me I will follow,
Where He leads me I will follow,
I'll go with Him, with Him all the way."

THE JOURNEY FORWARD:

How far will you follow Him today? Instead of a quick shower, might you have time to soak in a tub long enough for your fingers and toes to wrinkle? While relaxing, might you ask God to lead you in an area you haven't fully entrusted to Him?

# MEDICINE FOR THE MOUTH

## FROM A MOUSE

*M*y daughter has discovered Pez® candy. She calls them her "medicine." Alyssa is amazed at her own skill, having mastered the art of tipping the head of the Mickey Mouse dispenser back to catch the sweet surprise.

Unfortunately, her discovery quickly leads to a disappointment. Before we arrived home from The Dollar Store after running Saturday errands, she finished her treat. It's not that the candy was so yummy, it was just so much fun to eat "medicine" out of the mouth of a mouse.

WHAT COMES OUT OF THE MOUTH OF A MICKEY MOUSE PEZ dispenser is sweet. This prompts me to ask myself if the words that come out of my mouth are sweet–like Pez–or bitter like a putrid peanut. I want my words to have more in common with candy than a rotten nut. My tongue is in need of constant attention.

Recently I failed horribly when my new car refused to start. My hubby had already left for work and I was running late. I called the car dealership first. Then I called the 800 number I found in my glove box for roadside assistance.

They casually informed me it would be over an hour before they could send anyone my way. The first person they sent couldn't help me. A dozen texts, five phone calls and another mechanic later, my car started. I was nearly five hours late.

This was a trial in controlling my tongue. While I didn't spew on a person, I spewed plenty of hate on my car. And yes, I did use the word "hate." The Pez candy dispenser sat upright in my cup dispenser to witness the shocking barrage.

Interestingly, I correct my children when they carelessly use the word "hate." And earlier in the week I had read and high-lighted in *Proverbs 13:3 the cautionary warning that:

"Careful words make for a careful life;
    careless talk may ruin everything."

I've seen words destroy families, relationships and friend-ships. They can destroy trust. Perhaps this is why, in James 3:6, we're told that the tongue is like a flame of fire. Like a whole world of wickedness, it can corrupt our entire body and set our whole life on fire.

As Christians you and I are called to be careful handling our words, just as we would be careful handling a flame. We are called to plant kernels of kindness with our words rather than seeds of strife.

I have learned so much from James. He reminds us that peacemakers reap a "harvest of righteousness" (James 3:18). This prompts me to ask myself what sort of harvest I'm reaping from the words I've planted. Do my words wound or heal?

Are they words that I'll be proud to have repeated when I stand before God? I know that there are words I regret saying immediately after I speak them. They aren't words that build up, but rather they tear down. We're told to let everything we say be "good and helpful, so that your words will be an encouragement to those who hear them" (Ephesians 4:29).

As Christians we are called to be like Christ, who was full of grace. Jesus explains that we all will give an account on judgment day for *every* idle word we speak. Words that come out of our mouth mirror what's in our heart (Matthew 12:35-37).

Yet, there were certainly times in scripture when Jesus spoke harsh words to those needing correction. Jesus did not tolerate hypocrisy, calling out the religious leaders again and again (Matt. 3:7, 23:1-36, 12:34, Luke 3:7, Luke 11:46, Acts 15:20, Gal. 6:13.).

He used strong, descriptive words calling these leaders snakes, blind guides, fools, hypocrites, whitewashed tombs and sons of vipers...just to name a few.

Jesus demonstrated righteous anger toward those who

oppressed others. Following His example, we too may be called to stand up against oppressors.

The challenge for me is to reserve my anger and harsh words for those times and circumstances that warrant it. I need the Holy Spirit within me to help me control my temper and my tongue. Sometimes I carelessly let anger choose my verbs and adjectives, demanding the last word.

For me it seems that Jesus used His words to free others from oppression…not to subject them to more oppression. Even more than asking myself, "What would Jesus do?" I find myself asking, "What would Jesus say?" Each day the answer is different.

On our journey together, we have turned to scripture every day as we look for **Diamonds In Our Days**. As we draw near the last leg of our journey, let's snuggle up closer to our Savior. Though our journey together in this book will end, our journey with Jesus is still in its beginning stages and will continue throughout eternity.

I want my heart to be filled with good so that even when bad things happen (like a contrary car starter) good comes out of my mouth. God is much more concerned about our hearts than even our words.

He knows it all starts in the heart. I have a long way to go and verses like those found in Psalm 119:11 tell me to "hide God's word in my heart" so that I won't sin against Him. Hiding God's word in our heart transforms us into people that reflect Him.

I'm friends with a retired pastor and his wife, Rick and Carla Jordan, who view every outing as a "mini mission trip." When they go shopping, they look for opportunities to minister to others in small ways with their words…

complimenting a custodian for their diligence…

encouraging a mom struggling with whiny kids…

thanking a cashier for their smile…

praising a waitress for her promptness…

cheering on a child who is opening the door for others.

They understand the truth of Proverbs 16:24:"Kind words are like honey–sweet to the soul and healthy for the body."

## THE JOURNEY FORWARD:

While you may not eat candy you call your "medicine" out of the mouth of a mouse named Mickey, can you transform someone's day from mundane to memorable with sweet words, warming their heart? On your journey forward, might you make it your goal to look for a person whom you can bless each day with kind words?

# TWO THUMBS CROSSED

*W*hen I was in pharmacy school, I donated blood often. The medical center was my second home. And while I disliked needles (and still do to this day), I grew accustomed to them. You can say we had a love-hate relationship.

Often as students we were asked to participate in medical experiments. Can I ask you to participate in a simple experiment that doesn't involve needles and only takes three seconds? Here we go.

Just fold your hands, as if you were in prayer. Now interlock your fingers folding them together and look down at your thumbs. Is your right thumb crossed over your left thumb or is your left thumb crossed over your right thumb? Easy peasy, right?

If you're a person that normally positions your right thumb over your left, change the way you interlock your thumbs and fingers. Does that feel incredibly awkward? If you can fold your hand either way comfortably, you're a rare gem, as less than one percent of the population has no preference.[1]

You and I spend a lifetime perfecting how we fold our hands in prayer. Have you ever wondered why we are 100% consistent in how we position each of our eight fingers and two thumbs?

Plain and simple. We each have different sides of our brains that are dominant. Even the tiniest of changes in this routine can feel strange.

MORE IMPORTANT THAN THE QUESTION OF **HOW** WE FOLD OUR hands in prayer is **if** we pray every day. Concerning prayer, you and I are told in 1 Thessalonians 5:17 very simply to: "Never stop praying."

That's three words and it's nearly the shortest verse in the Bible. I like Paul's straightforward approach. He doesn't complicate it. Likewise, Jesus kept it simple when He told us to find a peaceful place where we can be alone with God, where others can't see or hear us. There we are to be honest with God, sharing our hearts. God sees what we do privately and will "reward" us (Matthew 6:6). Having a preschool daughter, even a whisper of a reward brings a hush to our household. I too notice rewards and I look forward to them.

I like how The Message Bible shares that: "the focus will shift from you to God, and you will begin to sense his grace. The world is full of so-called prayer warriors who are prayer-ignorant.

They're full of formulas and programs and advice, peddling techniques for getting what you want from God" (Matthew 6:6-7). We're told not to fall for these foolish ideas, because our Father knows us better than we know ourselves. He knows exactly what we need. Prayer helps us walk in His Will.

Each time we pray the "Our Father," we're praying that God's Will for our lives be done (Matt 6:9-13). We're asking for the grace to walk in His Will, for strength and direction. And we appeal to God, asking that He leads us away from temptation. When we align our will with His will, God can redirect us away from evil pitfalls.


THE JOURNEY FORWARD:

How we habitually fold our hands in prayer (right thumb over left or left thumb over right) isn't important to God, but our habit of prayer is extremely important to Him. In Psalm 141:2 we're told that God remembers our prayer conversations as though they are a sweet-smelling perfume. Based on this scripture, might you have perfume (or aftershave) that you could spray on yourself as a reminder to "pray unceasingly"?

On our journey forward today, consider what might help you build a more Biblical prayer life. Because I knew a peaceful place to pray would help me focus, writing this chapter led me to declutter. What once was a closet built into the eaves has been transformed into a tranquil prayer hideaway.

# SPIRITUAL DYSLEXIA

*A*ixelsyd. You may not see this word everyday though you've definitely heard about it. In fact you probably know several people who have it...like the actor, Tom Cruise. On screen Cruise may "cruise" through movies like Mission Impossible, but in real life he doesn't "cruise" through books because reading for him is like an impossible mission.

Aixelsyd is dyslexia spelled backward. Cruise has dyslexia so words appear backwards making reading, spelling and writing more complicated. Kids like Cruise are often smart and hardworking. They just have trouble connecting the letters they see to the sounds those letters make. It affects up to one in ten people and is linked back to genes, which is why it often runs in families.[1]

WHILE MY KIDDOS DON'T STRUGGLE WITH DYSLEXIA, THEY'VE inherited a form of "spiritual dyslexia" from me. I sometimes get spiritual priorities backward. Actually, it runs in God's family.

Perhaps that's why this morning when reading my Bible I noticed that **live** written backwards spells **evil**. In the Bible we can read story after story about those who **live** with priorities that are backward. **Evil** backs into them like a car backing out of a parking space into a pedestrian.

Today I also realized adding a "d" to the beginning of **evil** gives us the word **devil**. In the beginning in the Garden of Eden, the **devil** tempted Eve to sample the forbidden fruit, forever complicating how humankind has **lived**. This brings us full circle, as **lived** written backward spells **devil**. The devil is the author of backward priorities.

We can look backward in time and find the **devil lived** in Judas Iscariot, who had backward priorities in a garden. This time it wasn't the Garden of Eden but the Garden of Gethsemane. The night Judas betrayed Jesus with a kiss, something normally given in love was grossly twisted.

Even today evil can twist and slither into our lives when our priorities are backward. That's exactly what happened, not in a garden in Jerusalem but in a camp in Mugunga. Today I read a letter from my dear friend, Cyndi Scarlett, who works for the US government with refugees in Africa. In it she writes about where she saw **evil live**:

Last Sunday, there was a tragedy in the camp where I work that reinforced why I am here. Two men were fighting. One took a machete and cut the ear off of the other. He ran away.

The one with the lost ear couldn't catch him. So what did he do in retaliation? He went to the home of the other man, took his baby from his wife's arms and beheaded it. This while people were watching.

Savagery.

The devil is alive and well in Mugunga. There has to be someone here who can show these people that there's a better way to live. If not me, then who? The rest of the world has forgotten this place.

This modern-day story of a severed ear takes me back to the Biblical story of a severed ear. Like the man in Cyndi's camp, Peter also severed a man's ear. The night Judas betrayed Jesus with a twisted kiss, Peter let his emotions lead rather than following his Lord's lead. Sometimes I too let my emotions lead, thinking my intentions make it all okay.

Instead of allowing evil to spiral out of control, Jesus lovingly took control and picked up the ear, miraculously reattaching it. Then Jesus reminded Peter that those who live by the sword will also die by the sword (Matthew 26:52). God's kingdom is advanced by faith not force (or nagging). This is a lesson I'm still learning...a lesson I've gotten backwards more times than I care to share.

Jesus was being taken captive by a mob of men with clubs and torches. The leading priests and Pharisees had also given Judas a contingent of armed Roman soldiers and temple guards (John 18:3). The apostles were sorely outnumbered. Jesus knew exactly what was going to happen, but He kept faith in front, not allowing force to lead.

Put me in that situation and I would use force or run and hide, but Jesus didn't. Rather He calmly stepped forward and asked, "Who are you searching for?" This makes me sad because that's the same question that Jesus still calmly asks me when I'm looking to the others (or even things) for fulfillment.

The mob in the Garden of Gethsemane was looking for a man, "Jesus from Nazareth," but Who they found was infinitely more. Jesus stepped forward giving them another opportunity to see Him for Who He really was-God incarnate. What happened next in John 18:6 takes my breathe away:

"As Jesus said 'I AM he,'
**they ALL drew back and fell to the ground!"**

I am awed by this detail and left to wonder. Why did this powerful mob all fall? Time and time again we hear that Jesus spoke with power and authority (Matthew 7:28-29, Luke 4:32). This was one of those times for sure!

Were they shocked by His authority and His answer? Unashamedly, Jesus was proclaiming His divinity with this "I AM" statement. It may not seem obvious to us, but it was Windex® clear to anyone who was Jewish! They understood that

Jesus was declaring Himself to be God. His Father first spoke these words in Exodus 3:14 identifying Himself by the name, "I AM."

Did the mob sense Christ's power and fall in awe? I believe they did. I say this knowing that there will be a day when "every knee will bow" (Romans 14:11, Phil. 2:10-11). Agnostics and atheists may be the most floored that their legs give way.

I ask myself if I was part of the scene, where would I be? Would I be like Peter acting in love but misled by emotion... fighting in fear rather than functioning in faith?

Likely, I would be one of the ten disciples who fell asleep despite being asked to keep watch with Jesus as He prayed for strength. I've been known to fall asleep when I pray.

It was the middle of the night and it had been a hectic, emotionally draining Passover week. Jerusalem was packed wall-to-wall with fellow Jews. The fickle crowds had turned against Jesus, but was this really the end? With my tummy full and my eyelids heavy, I could easily see myself asking these weighty questions and being dumbfounded, wondering if it was all a bad dream.

Peter didn't understand what Jesus meant when He said that His hour of darkness had come. He was a man who knew lots about fishing and little about fighting. In that dark moment he didn't care about prophecy being fulfilled. Peter just didn't want Jesus to be hurt. Dare I say, faith was in the back seat when Peter figuratively stepped on the gas.

I can relate to Peter...can't we all? Like Peter, I too lash out and lose focus. I get angry fast and listen last. I act on feelings rather than standing on faith. I figuratively try to stop a battalion of **armed soldiers** by slicing the ear off of an **unarmed servant** when I...

- look to my successes to gauge my value rather than my position as God's child...
- look to my failures to confirm my worst fears rather than giving those fears to my Father...
- shop to fill my closet with new pieces rather than pray to fill my mind with His peace...
- depend on my children to give me purpose rather than on my Savior...
- turn to food as my friend to satisfy deeper soul cravings...
- depend on Facebook to tell me how well I'm "liked" rather than resting in God's love.

Like Peter, I lash out at those closest to me. It's quite likely the servant was the nearest person to Peter. Maybe Peter's goal was to sever the servant's head, but the guy was agile and bent to the side to avoid the blade.

Unfortunately, over 2,000 years later, an African man about the same age as Peter wasn't so fortunate and had his ear sliced off. Never having known the story of Jesus, the refugee retaliated in anger. Though this man is responsible for his actions, it makes me think…might we as a church be called to tell those like him about the Good News of Christ? I believe we are.

Moments before Jesus ascended into heaven, He commissioned us each to make disciples of all nations. He told us to baptize others in the name of the Father and of the Son and of the Holy Spirit and to teach others to obey His commands. Then Jesus assures us that He will be with us always, "even to the very end of the age" (Mathew 28:19-20). These were His last words before leaving this Earth.

Last words are precious, aren't they? I remember every syllable of the last words of my family members perfectly. I even remember the tone and the expression on their face when they spoke them.

I imagine Jesus' eyes were smiling, filled with tears of joy knowing He was headed home to His Dad, yet sad that He was leaving His dearest friends. His tone was certainly one that spoke volumes of His Love for us.

Jesus is with you and me as we share the Good News. Which brings us back to Cyndi's question: "There has to be someone here who can show these people that there is a better way to live. If not me, then who?" A severed ear led to an innocent baby boy dying. Our sin led to an innocent baby boy being born so He could die for us.

This brings us back to the beginning of this dyslexic chapter. There is hope in Christ. **Evil** spelled backward is **live,** but if one single vowel is changed, **live** becomes **love.** By reattaching a severed ear, Jesus showed us how to resist **evil** and **live** in **love**. We too can defeat **evil** when we **live** in **love!**

## THE JOURNEY FORWARD

As we round the last bend on this expedition, might you say a silent prayer for those people who struggle with dyslexia? And might you pray for strength and wisdom for times you and others (like the African refugee that resorted to violence) may struggle with spiritual dyslexia?

Together on this journey, let's keep our eyes focused forward and fixed on Jesus, "the author and finisher of our faith (Hebrews 12:2)". He can help us do more than read well. After the last page of this book is closed, He can help us write our stories well!

# A COMMON COLD

$\mathscr{A}$s we near the end of our journey, let's look back. In this book our journey started with the first snow of the season captured on the cover. Do you remember the times you wrapped your little ones like mummies with scarves and hats while warning "You need to bundle up or you'll catch a cold?"

Millions of moms have uttered these words as their children head out the door. Coats zipped to their chins and hoods drawn tight with mittens in place, we think we have protected our kiddos from that nasty but common ailment that we've nicknamed "a cold." But have we?

Despite common belief, *having a cold* has nothing whatsoever to do with *being in the cold.* In fact cold, dry winter air is less conducive for sharing contagious germs than warm, humid summer air.

So why are we more susceptible in the winter? It's not the

cold **outside** that is the direct cause of the problem. It's the cold
that drives us **inside**, where we're more likely to share germs. A
cold is caused by bacteria (in most cases by Homophiles influenza
or streptococcus) that are passed from person to person by sneez-
ing, shaking hands or drinking after one another.

JUST AS WE MAY BELIEVE THAT BEING BUNDLED UP IS GOING TO
keep us safe from a cold, we may believe that if our good deeds
outweigh our bad deeds, we'll earn heaven. Yet God tells us that
it's not by our works but by God's grace that we're saved.

Eugene Peterson, author of The Message Bible, says it this
way: "Saving is all his idea, and all his work. All we do is trust
him enough to let him do it. It's God's gift from start to finish! We
don't play the major role. If we did, we'd probably go around
bragging that we'd done the whole thing! No, we neither make
nor save ourselves. God does both the making and saving" (*Ephesians 2:8-9).

Salvation is a gift. Gifts are given; they're not something we
earn. And we don't pay for them. Yet when it comes to salvation–
the greatest gift of all–we expect strings to be attached. We can't
fathom that faith alone could save us.

We feel as if we have to work for salvation. Maybe this is
because it's easier to believe in something we can see. Like
microscopic germs are not visible (to the naked eye), faith is not
visible (to the naked eye). So we focus on things we can see.

We can see gloves and coats. Similarly, we can see deeds and works.

I've heard it said that "religion" will keep more people from heaven than anything else. Though this sounds like a paradox, if **acting religious outwardly** becomes more important to us than **knowing Christ inwardly**, this could be true.

People who are religious **outwardly** but have not accepted Christ **inwardly** are like those who don coats and gloves to avoid catching the cold. While these practices keep us warm and make us feel safe, they don't protect us from germs.

The apostle Paul emphasizes that no one can ever be made right with God by doing what the law commands. The law simply shows us how sinful we are (Romans 3:20). Paul wrote this to believers in Rome, who had been confused by "legalism," which is what my dad would call "a fancy, five-letter-word" for putting the law above grace.

Legalism adds legal requirements beyond faith in Christ. It seems the early church struggled with legalism, just like we do today. Paul clarifies the issue again to believers in Galatia explaining that a person is made right with God by faith in Jesus, **not by obeying the law** (Galatians 2:16).

I think the reason Paul restates this message multiple times is because he knew how foundational it was (and still is) to understand that salvation is a gift. My Dad always said, "**In this world** there's no such thing as a free lunch." But when it comes to the gift of salvation, it's **out of this world** and it's truly free.

Our living faith and love for Christ transforms us...resulting in love for others. I grew up singing "They'll know we are Christians by our love, by our love. Yes. They'll know we are Christians by our love."[1]

This is how our faith becomes visible to a world craving love. It's what James was talking about when he said, "Show me your faith **without** your works and I will show you my faith **by** my works." (James 2:18)

Together as members of Christ's universal church we can be known by our love that germinates from a deep, living faith in Christ. Together we can accomplish more than we can individually.

Together we can encourage one another. So while going to church on Sundays can't save us, it can help us come to a saving faith. The church can also provide us with opportunities to live out our faith.

We can't be everything to everyone. Individually we don't have the time, talent and training. But collectively, we do. As the church, we are Christ's hands and feet on this earth (John 14:12).

Today "organized religion" is often seen in a negative light with less people attending church than in previous generations. Interestingly, younger generations applaud "spirituality."[2] Each generation has their unique perspective and God loves each generation.

How we "practice" our faith may change. Bands may replace choirs. Jeans may replace dresses. Online giving may replace collection plates. But the message of salvation is unchanging and is needed by every generation. We will forever be saved by our Savior...not by our own works.

We are sinners. We are also Christ's church. It's easy to understand why the world can look at us and see our shortcomings. Jesus saw and understood our shortcomings. What He could not understand or tolerate was our pride made visible by our hypocrisy.

Hypocrisy gives "organized religion" a bad name and rightfully so. But imperfections in the church can also be used as an excuse to avoid church altogether. Christ encourages us to gather as a body of believers.

Faith unites us. So while the act of going to church on Sundays cannot save us, the faith that comes from hearing God's Word pointing us to Christ does save us (Romans 10:17).

THE JOURNEY FORWARD:

Being exposed to bacteria results in the common cold...not being exposed to the cold temperature. Being exposed to and accepting Christ results in our salvation...not just trying to be good and do good. On our journey forward today, is there someone in your family or circle of friends that needs to be exposed to the contagious love of Christ's saving grace?

# WINDOWS OF OPPORTUNITY

My father has a fun-loving sense of humor. He also has a debilitating disease. Dad has advanced Parkinson's Disease with dementia yet he still makes us laugh doing what he has dubbed "the Parkinson's shuffle." It's an awkward hillbilly jig that ends with a ba dum chh drum roll and dad adding: "I've always been a mover and a shaker." It's his way of showing he won't allow the disease to plunder his joy.

Parkinson's has been dubbed "the shaking palsy." It's progressive with a hallmark tremor. Too much crazy movement with medicine or too little controlled movement without medicine. It's a high wire balancing act.

Patients like my dad are commonly frozen stiff, not able to move even though their brain is telling their body to step on the gas. That's why it's described by neurologists as a movement disorder. Dad—forever a Mr. Fix It—simply says he has "short-circuited." He can tell his legs to move but there's a "delayed obedience" from his limbs. Dad always taught us kids that "delayed obedience" was a "cousin to disobedience."

Inertia is his arch enemy. Once he starts moving, it's hard for him to stop. Falling has become as common as the old Levis® he wears.

Dad is a "man's man" who always gave more than he took and taught us to do the same. Even when things were tight, he and my mom were generous beyond their means. It's hard for him to accept help.

I live nearly six hours away, so I call home daily. My dad, who could once figure out everything from leaky faucets to creaky floors, now struggles with the phone. While he still recognizes my voice and can understand me, his speech is slurred and it's nearly impossible for me to understand him. He can't think of the right word, and when he does, he can't get it out before the word becomes lost then tossed like last night's salad.

Conversation is exhausting for him. He's embarrassed because in his mind he knows what he wants to say. My mom helps him so he can still be included. She's so thoughtful.

Even with medicine, simple tasks like fastening his pants, buttoning his shirt and putting on his shoes have become impossible without my mom's help. Once very active in the community, cooking at the soup kitchen and delivering communion to the sick, Mom doesn't leave dad alone anymore.

At night when she's asleep, my dad becomes a prisoner in his own bed. He describes it as feeling pinned down like a bug to a cork-board in an insect collection. I've bought the lightest feather blanket I can find. Even still Dad says covers "bury him alive" as he becomes tangled and feels strangled.

Dad—a man who doesn't like change—doesn't like that now his box springs and mattress rest directly on new, thick carpet mom had installed to cushion his falls. Dad wants everything to stay the same…but this disease marches on with no mercy.

In early stages my dad's mind was still agile, but now his brain stalls and everything goes blank like a car that runs out of gas in the middle of a busy intersection. Each day the battle becomes more difficult…and more exasperating.

Even still, Dad is grateful. He will be the first to tell you that he's had a good life and God has blessed him more than he deserves. He was always a pillar of strength when I was a puddle of tears.

Our whole family is thankful for modern medicine as it has offered a window of opportunity over the past decade. Dad has been taking neurotransmitter replacement therapy. This helps treat his symptoms.

While it has stalled the inevitable, there is no cure. Though the medicines fight to keep the window open, more and more drug is needed offering smaller and smaller bits of relief.

What's so amazing is that daily as a pharmacist I am able to work with doctors to help treat those with this disease. The goal is to replace the neurotransmitter (dopamine) that patients lack, in order to keep them functioning as long as possible. Doctors strive to keep the windows of opportunity open for their patients.

As I've watched my Dad struggle with the simplest of tasks, I think about my spiritual "window of opportunity" to shape eternity. Each day here on earth I have opportunities. Like me, I imagine you want your life to make a difference.

I long for purpose. Seeing my dad struggle and realizing that time is a gift, I want to use my years wisely. the Bible tells us that we can speak with human eloquence but without love we're nothing but a creaking door. We can teach God's Word with power, understanding scripture and making everything plain as day, but if we don't love, our lives don't count. We're told that we can even have mountain-moving faith, but if we don't love others in the end we have nothing to show for all that faith. Even if we give everything to the poor, including our lives serving others twenty-four-seven, but don't love, we've gotten nowhere. Love is the greatest gift we can have and can give (1 Corinthians 13:1-3, 12-13).

Through love we can reach others. Even those with hearts that seem as hard as diamonds need love. While people may not think they need the Good News of the gospels, we all need good news, don't we?

It's Good News to know that someone cares for us and will listen to us. It's Good News to know that we matter. It's Good News to know that God loves us so much He sent His Son so that whoever believes is saved (John 3:16).

Just like my dad with Parkinson's, the inertia to get moving is the hardest part. Small acts of kindness can open the door for you and me to share our story and what Jesus means to us. By nature, I'm not a brave person but even I can share:

A smile for another while waiting in a not-so-express line.

A hug when a friend at work looks exhausted.

A to-go hot cup of coffee on a cold day for the mailman.

A compliment for the lady in the elevator who is wearing an outfit that she makes look great. Kindness can make our day. If you're thinking something or someone looks nice, say it. I have never had anyone get mad over a well-meaning compliment. It brightens their day and lightens their load!

You may be the first one to share a glimpse of good news in the form of a compliment. It's possible that you're the first person to listen to their story. In time you or another person may be able to share how much God loves them and wants them to spend eternity in heaven. After all, Jesus came to save us from ourselves. We each need our Savior. And if we're transparent, we each have times we need saved too...

Times when we are locked out of our cars...

Times when we have forgotten our wallet at home...

Times when we have an unmanageable deadline or...

Times when we need help with our unmanageable kiddos.

You may be living right now in a time of need. God allows us each to experience difficult times so that we better understand the hard times of others. These trials give us dimension allowing us to be multifaceted. Giving us depth and clarity...like a diamond.

Being able to relate and reach out to others is part of how God uses the bad things to work them into good things (Romans 8:28). Suffering alone for the sake of suffering makes no sense, but suffering that helps others gives our lives great purpose.

So in the end we have the window of opportunity to share God's love and to help others come to know our Savior. Our window of opportunity is now.

THE JOURNEY FORWARD:

As you button your shirt and tie your shoes today, might you thank God for your health and being able to move freely? More-over, might you thank God for your window of opportunity to love others. Reach through the window and offer a hand to someone who is in need. You could be the diamond in their day!

## KILEY'S COURAGE

We started this journey with the courageous story of Sophia–the sweet, young lady who was engaged to be married. After her lupus diagnosis, Sophia found herself with a gown but no groom. I like romantic endings. So it seems fitting to end our journey with the inspiring story of a sweet, young lady named Kiley.

Both Sophia and Kiley are stunningly beautiful. Both have flawless complexions and bright white smiles. They each are tall and slender. And both have an illness for which there is no cure.

Kiley has Glioblastoma Multiforme (GBM), the most aggressive form of brain cancer.[1] Although GBM is not thought to be inherited, Kiley's father was diagnosed with it a few months before she had brain surgery to remove her golf ball-sized tumor.

Kiley has four sisters and a Godly mom. Her church family has also rallied around her. Kiley inspires others to be brave sharing their faith in Jesus. On her CaringBridge account she writes: "If more people come to know Christ by how I live, then let me live. If more people come to know Christ by my death, then take me home. If more people come to know Christ thru my suffering, then let me suffer."[2]

These are words that are easy to write when life is sparkling. But when chemotherapy claims your hair, could we speak these words with confidence? At eighteen, Kiley is the bravest young lady I know.

As I type, my eyes leak but Kiley isn't looking for tears. She's looking for others whom she can help. "Before my brain surgery and diagnosis, I thought that no cancer would be 'the miracle.' We expect so many things from God but He moves in miraculous ways."

Kiley is so right even when cancer is so wrong. She trusts Jesus with her life and wants you to trust Him to save you...to give you hope and a future. Kiley is radiant as she explains: "Telling others about Jesus fills me." When interviewing her for this book, I asked how she so bravely shares Jesus. She reassured me: "God brings opportunities to share Jesus when you least expect it. He will give you the words and the wisdom." Kiley reminds us, "None of us know how long we have." She urges us to "Live life with the end in mind."

Kiley loves life and a young man named Cole. Soon after her diagnosis, they attended the homecoming dance together. Kiley rocked a little black dress that she paired with satin red pumps. She beamed as she explained how blessed she felt to have found both on sale.

Like the pair of pumps she snagged, Kiley understands first-hand that often here on Earth joy is paired with sorrow, success with setbacks, and life with loss. In the midst of her battle, Kiley radiates hope & beauty. And she has some exciting news!

Cole proposed and she accepted.

Then she went shopping with her mom and said "yes to the dress." So now she has both a gown and a groom.

We too have a Bridegroom who is faithful. He promises to never leave us or forsake us. We will never have to face our fears alone. He will be with us for better or for worse…for richer or for poorer…in sickness and in health…to love and to cherish. And that's just the beginning because our Bridegroom will be with us far beyond "until do us part."

Like Cole who will be beaming and waiting for Kiley as she walks down the aisle, our Bridegroom is beaming and waiting for us. Someday we will see Him face to face. That's a day we can anticipate with joy, just as Kiley anticipates her wedding day.

**The Journey Forward:**

So as we end our journey to discover Diamonds In Our Days, like Kiley can we "live life with the end in mind"? The biggest most beautiful wedding feast ever is being planned by Jesus, our Bridegroom.

At our wedding reception in heaven, we will be more stunning than the Hope Diamond. We will be perfect. Radiant and flawless. Shimmering for our Savior. He promises us that in heaven we will live happily ever after. If Kiley and Sophia can trust Him for the perfect ending, we certainly can too!

# MY JOURNEY FORWARD

## A DIAMOND LOST

*I* love to sit in uncomfortable chairs and wait. My doctor's waiting room is my absolute favorite place to spend time." Said no one ever!

Waiting is hard. And waiting rooms are a hard place to be left when our mind is swirling with questions. Even still, I've learned lots of lessons while waiting, praying and trusting. While waiting is hard, together we've learned that hard in God's hands produces diamonds!

For twenty-five years I waited and prayed. During all those years God gave me the same answer. "No." Well, actually it was more of a "no, not yet." But years of "not yet" feel a lot like a "no."

"Lord, will you help me publish my books? I don't know where to start. Will you guide me? Could you use these books to bless others?" No's are hard. But we are told to keep asking and praying (Mathew 7:7). And, I kept journaling and writing.

God's answer was clear. I was not to pursue publishing until my children were grown. Alyssa and Garrett were my first priority. And my husband did not support me leaving my paying job as a pharmacist. A ministry in writing and speaking made no financial sense.

Years passed. I focused on my family and counted each blessing. In His kindness God opened doors with my church calling me to teach Sunday school to teens for twenty years. Those high school students were like **Diamonds in my Days** then and now as they are young adults raising their own families.

When church leadership transitioned me from young adults to women's ministry, I cried...quite literally. Every time I attended a service, I wept. One Sunday I sobbed so hard my own daughter gave me "the look." Her face told me she thought I was losing it. And I was. I was losing a youth ministry that had become a huge part of my life.

Looking back, now I see that God was preparing me for a faith expedition. Having just completed an exciting journey of our own in this book, we know that God can take all things and work them into beautifully brilliant things...like diamonds.

When our Director of Women's Ministry retired, I was asked to co-chair women's ministries. God moved me to write Bible studies and lead women's retreats. Along the way church elders asked me to chair our hospitality team comprised mostly of women.

There was a need and God invited me to fill it. When we say yes to God, even in hard things, He honors our yes and returns blessings that are so abundant they spill over on others (Luke 6:38). I want my blessing bowl like I want my popcorn bowl— brimming over.

The reason I share my journey is to highlight that God is a faithful Artisan. For twenty-five years He told me to wait. Then quite abruptly, the year my nest was empty while I was still working as a pharmacist in industry, God brought a friend into my path who was an author. Literally He had her walk right up to me at a medical conference.

She shared her journey and then shared her contact information. That was what I call a God moment. Jonna offered to help guide me on a God-ordained journey of my own. My husband did not object.

I would love to tell you my ministry path has been paved with diamonds ever since. It has not. God's ways are not always our ways (Isaiah 55:8). But just as you and I have learned in this book, the hard path can lead to beauty. My first book launch was the biggest planned social event in my life, second only to my wedding.

The church hall was reserved. My first shipment of 500 books arrived. Invitations were sent. Baristas were booked. Food was ordered. And family was set to arrive from several states.

Then came the blizzard.

It was a full-blown snowstorm with high winds and low visibility. This snow was the first of the season and hit much harder than expected. The day before it was a balmy sixty degrees. No coats required.

It seemed decades of dreams were a dreary disappointment. The day slid downhill, picking up speed like a sled. My mother became violently ill with the twenty-four-hour flu, though she had traveled 600 miles for my big day. My frail father fell outside Walmart when on their way. Thanks to an agile, young man who literally scooped him up and laid him across the front seat of the car, my dad was there. Only some family and few of my closest friends ventured out that treacherous day.

And just when it seemed things couldn't grow any worse, they did. Once home I realized a diamond from my tennis bracelet was missing. But with a house full of guests, the bracelet was laid aside.

That night I didn't sleep. In my mind I retraced every step. Vaguely I remembered catching my arm on a stack of food pallets when racing up the back stairs to the pulpit to preach. I had taken a shortcut down a remote hallway past our community food pantry. Thinking back, I felt sure that's where my diamond was torn from my bracelet.

On Monday when the roads were cleared, I said goodbye to my guests and sped to church. When I arrived, to my shock, every pallet had been relocated outside to the frozen parking lot by volunteers for reasons unknown to me.

There were ice crystals strewn everywhere as far as my eyes could see. You've heard of finding a needle in a haystack. Try locating a lost diamond among a million frozen ice crystals! I wanted to sit on the curb and cry.

I would love to tell you my lost diamond was found that morning. It was not. I would also love to report that I sold enough books to meet my ministries stretch goal of $10,000 to be donated to a charity that helps those who are victims of natural disasters.

Without eyes of faith it would seem that my loss—the cost of my diamond—exceeded my ministry's gain. But we have learned that the hard journey, when taken with God, can lead to beauty (2 Cor. 4:17). The story of my ministry was only beginning to be written by God. He's the Master Author. I've read His Book and know that His endings are brilliant.

Lifting our hands and praising God when life is good is easy. But lifting our hands and praising God when life is hard, well… that's hard. Yet even in hard things, we can trust that God is faithful (Psalm 100:5).

The lesson from the blizzard that day still speaks volumes to me of God's love. Just as snow covers the world's imperfections, Christ covers our imperfections making us as white as snow (Isa. 1:18, Psalm 51:7).

Snow makes Jesus visible to the world. He is the visible image of our invisible God (Col. 1:15). He is God incarnate. God's perfect gift wrapped in skin.

His story is the history of all humankind. We chose sin over Him. He chose us over everything comfortable. And now our sin is cleansed by Him, through the blood of His sacrificial death (1

John 1:7-9, Hebrews 9:14, Revelation 1:5, 14). So in the end, hard doesn't destroy us and sin doesn't win. Christ has us covered...not just in winter with snow, but in every sickness and season of life.

On the cover of this book, my hands are lifted in praise. It's a natural response when we are given a glimmer of His glory. When we lift our hands to Him, He lifts us up and pulls us close, comforting us. I needed lifted up after my "Blown Away By A Blizzard Book Launch." It was a flop.

This expedition has shown us that even in hardships and sickness, He can teach us, take us and make us into diamonds that shine, helping others see His light (Matthew 5:16). We were created to bring God glory and we are most radiant when we shine for Him...like diamonds.

So when you start to question your value, lift your hands high and look to Him for assurance and help like a child would lift their hands when they need picked up. Then look around you for someone who needs a diamond in their day. You can be that diamond.

Always remember, you are beloved, brilliant and beautiful. There are millions of diamonds but only one you. And though you may have wintery seasons when you feel more like a forgotten lump of coal, know that you are cherished. Shine on dear friend. Shine on!

# ABOUT THE AUTHOR

Lisa Wilt is an inspirational speaker and author of multiple books. She was awarded the gold medal by Illumination Book Awards in 2019 and the silver medal in 2020. These awards honor the year's best new titles written and published with a Christian worldview. Past winners include Pope Francis, Desmond Tutu, Lysa Terkeurst and Anne Graham Lotz.

Lisa's one-minute W.O.W. Words, airs daily on the radio to lighten the load for those on the go. Her podcasts and blogs can be found on Life885.com. Lisa is founder and president of *Rx for the Soulful Heart*, a ministry to encourage weary people and worthy ministries, with all proceeds from her speaking and books being donated to charity. You can visit her at LisaWilt.com.

For over 32 years Lisa has worked full-time as an award-winning pharmacist in community pharmacy and the pharmaceutical industry. By grace, Lisa and her husband–a physician–have two grown children who have followed in their medical footpaths. Of all her accomplishments, the title that most defines Lisa is CHILD OF GOD. As her family will tell you, Lisa's weaknesses are thrift-store bargains and Cookie Dough Ice Cream.

~

- **Windows of Wonder**: Discovering Extraordinary W.O.W. Moments in the Ordinary
- **Glimmers of Glory**: Discovering God Moments in the Gloomy

Upcoming Books

- **Mirrors of Majesty**: Discovering Majestic Moments in the Mundane
- **Delight Drizzled Days:** Delighting in God and Discovering the Desires of Your Heart

~

# NOTES

## 3. INTRODUCTION

1. Griggs, Jessica. Diamond No Longer Nature's Hardest Material. NewScientist. https://www.newscientist.com/article/dn16610-diamond-no-longer-natures-hardest-material/ (accessed 2/23/2020)
2. Rodriguez, Tori. "Laugh Lots, Live Longer" Scientific American Mind. https://www.scientificamerican.com/article/laugh-lots-live-longer/ (accessed 2/21/2020)
3. Tsai, Lin-Wei. "Nanodiamonds for Medical Applications: Interaction with Blood in Vitro and in Vivo" Int J Mol Sci. 2016 Jul; 17(7): 1111 https://www.ncbi.nlm.nih.gov/pmc/articles/PMC4964486/ (accessed 2/22/2020)

## 4. A GOWN BUT NO GROOM

1. "What is Lupus?" Lupus Foundation of America, Lupus.org https://www.lupus.org/resources/what-is-lupus (accessed 3/4/2019)
2. Ziglar, Zig. Quotespedia.org https://www.quotespedia.org/authors/z/zig-ziglar/fear-has-two-meanings-forget-everything-and-run-or-face-everything-and-rise-the-choice-is-yours-zig-ziglar/ (accessed 2/20/2020)

## 5. RING AROUND MY FINGER

1. "Why Does My Gold Ring Turn My Finger Black?" YatesJewlers.com https://www.yatesjewelers.com/why-does-my-gold-ring-turn-my-finger-black.html (accessed 4/4/2019)

# 6. A BUTTERSCOTCH DISK

1. Enayati, Amanda "How Hope Can Help You Heal" CNN.com https://www.cnn.com/2013/04/11/health/hope-healing-enayati/index.html (accessed 3/3/2019)
2. Ibid.
3. ibid.
4. Guinness World Records Longest time breath held voluntarily (male) https://www.guinnessworldrecords.com/world-records/longest-time-breath-held-voluntarily-(male)? (accessed 2/24/2020)

# 9. THE ISLETS OF LANGERHANS

1. "The Pancreas and Its Functions" columbiasurgery.org https://columbiasurgery.org/pancreas/pancreas-and-its-functions (accessed 1/20/2020)
2. Chiang, Jane L., "Type 1 Diabetes in Children and Adolescents: A Position Statement by the American Diabetes Association" American Diabetes Association, http://care.diabetesjournals.org/content/41/9/2026 (accessed 3/3/2019)
3. "Mortality in Type 1 Diabetes" National Institute of Diabetes and Digestive and Kidney Disease, National Institutes of Health. Diabetes in America, 3rd Edition. https://www.niddk.nih.gov/about-niddk/strategic-plans-reports/diabetes-in-america-3rd-edition (accessed 1/17/2020)

# 11. GLUTEN & GRACE

1. "Sources of Gluten" Celiac Disease Foundation, Celiac.org, https://celiac.org/gluten-free-living/what-is-gluten/sources-of-gluten/ (accessed 3/3/2019)
2. "Slavery in the Roman World" Ancient History Encyclopedia, https://www.ancient.eu/article/629/slavery-in-the-roman-world/ (accessed 1/16/2020)

## 12. TRANSIENT ISCHEMIC ATTACKS

1. Mayo Clinic. "Transient Ischemic Attack (TIA)" mayoclinic.org https://www.mayoclinic.org/diseases-conditions/transient-ischemic-attack/diagnosis-treatment/drc-20355684 (accessed 3/3/2019)
2. "The Telltale Signs of Verbal Abuse" U.S. News and World Report. https://health.usnews.com/health-news/health-wellness/articles/2013/10/03/the-telltale-signs-of-verbal-abuse (accessed 3/15/2020)

## 13. RESTLESS LEGS

1. NIH National Institute of Neurological Disorders and Stroke "Restless Legs Syndrome Fact Sheet" ninds.nih.gov https://www.ninds.nih.gov/Disorders/Patient-Caregiver-Education/Fact-Sheets/Restless-Legs-Syndrome-Fact-Sheet (accessed 2/2/2020)
2. Luders, Eileen. "Why Sex Matters: Brain Size Independent Differences in Gray Matter Distributions between Men and Women" Journal of Neuroscience 2009 Nov 11:29(45): 14265-14270) https://www.ncbi.nlm.nih.gov/pmc/articles/PMC3110817/ (accessed 2/17/2020)

## 14. FAMOUS COUPLES

1. Bhatt, Jalpa. "Efficiency of intrauterine insemination (IUI) along with different ovarian stimulation protocols as a method of treating infertility" https://pdfs.semanticscholar.org/bc82/d73d584a9f9b5e90f6a1ec90b139577e3c98.pdf (accessed 2/17/2020)

## 17. INVISIBLE LIGHT

1. "Imagine the Universe" NASA National Aeronautics and Space Administration. imagine.gsfc.nasa.gov https://imagine.gsfc.nasa.gov/science/science.html (accessed 3/3/2019)

2. Mukamal, Reena "How Humans See Color" American Academy of Opthalmology https://www.aao.org/eye-health/tips-prevention/how-humans-see-in-color (accessed 3/1/2020)

## 20. MY FAVORITE COMFORT FOOD

1. "The World's Healthiest Foods" whfoods.org http://www.whfoods.com/genpage.php?tname=foodspice&dbid=48 (accessed 3/3/2019)

## 21. NOSE AND HAIR

1. "The Hair's Life Cycle" LaRoche-Posay.com https://www.laroche-posay.sg/article/Loss-Hair/a14032.aspx (accessed 3/3/2019)

## 22. REVIA®

1. Volpicelli, JR. "Naltrexone in the treatment of alcohol dependence." Arch Gen Psychiatry. 1992;49:76-80. https://www.ncbi.nlm.nih.gov/pubmed/1345133 (accessed 2/17/ 2020)

## 24. BELLY BUTTONS

1. Mike Ashcroft and Rachel Olsen, *My One Word* (Grand Rapids: Zondervan, 2012)

## 25. M & M'S

1. Johnson, Nicole Blair, MPH et.al. "CDC National Health Report: Leading Causes of Morbidity and Mortality and Associated Behavioral Risk and Protective Factors—United States, 2005–2013CDC" Centers for Disease Control and Prevention. CDC.gov https://www.cdc.gov/mmwr/preview/mmwrhtml/su6304a2.htm (accessed 3/3/2019)

## 26. FIBROMYALGIA

1. "Fibromyalgia: Symptoms and Causes" MayoClinic.org https://www. mayoclinic.org/diseases-conditions/fibromyalgia/symptoms-causes/syc-20354780 (accessed 2/17/2020)

## 28. PRUNEY WRINKLES

1. Blandy, Ernest. "Where He Leads Me." 1890. Hymnary.org (Assessed 12/10/2020)

## 30. TWO THUMBS CROSSED

1. McDonald, John H. "Myths of Human Genetics" University of Delaware, udel.edu http://udel.edu/~mcdonald/mythhandclasp.html (accessed 3/3/2019)

## 31. SPIRITUAL DYSLEXIA

1. "What is Dyslexia?" WebMD.com https://www.webmd.com/children/ understanding-dyslexia-basics (accessed 2/3/2020)

## 32. A COMMON COLD

1. Father Peter Scholtes "They'll Know We Are Christians By Our Love." 1968, A1, They'll Know We are Christians By Our Love, F.E.L. Records, 1968, vinyl.
2. "In U.S., Decline of Christianity Continues at Rapid Pace" PewForum.org https://www.pewforum.org/2019/10/17/in-u-s-decline-of-christianity-continues-at-rapid-pace/ (accessed 1/25/2020)

# 34. KILEY'S COURAGE

1. "What is GBM" National Foundation for Cancer Research. https://www.nfcr.org/gbm-agile/what-is-gbm/ (accessed October 31, 2020)
2. CaringBridge.org    https://www.caringbridge.org/visit/kileydaniels/journal (accessed October 31, 2020)

Made in the USA
Middletown, DE
10 May 2021

39452441R00119